STRUCTURES OF
CHRISTIAN
PRIESTHOOD

STRUCTURES OF CHRISTIAN PRIESTHOOD

*A study of home, marriage, and celibacy
in the pastoral service of the church*

JEAN-PAUL AUDET

TRANSLATED BY ROSEMARY SHEED

THE MACMILLAN COMPANY · NEW YORK

Library of Congress Catalog Card Number: 67-31350

First American Edition 1968

Nihil obstat: John Coventry SJ
Imprimatur: ✠Patrick Casey, Vic. Gen.
Westminster, 10th July, 1967
The Nihil obstat and Imprimatur are a declaration that
a book or pamphlet is considered to be free from doctrinal
or moral error. It is not implied that those who have
granted the Nihil obstat and Imprimatur agree with the
contents, opinions, or statements expressed.

The Macmillan Company, New York
Collier-Macmillan Canada Ltd., Toronto Ontario

Printed in the United States of America

Contents

Contents

Preface

THIS LITTLE BOOK has grown out of circumstances. It began as an attempt to give some advice wanted by an individual; and of its first aims, the one it has kept above all is that of going straight to the heart of the problem, without sacrificing either clarity or a balanced view on the altar of brevity.

Thus, especially, in the apparatus of references, I have restricted myself to mentioning only the earliest sources. Even among these, there has been more than one case where a choice has had to be made; and when it seemed to me necessary to choose, I was chiefly guided by the somewhat restricted point of view with which I began, as well as by the relative importance of each witness in the totality of the historical situation to which he belonged. I realize only too well that such a proceeding involves risk—but from the moment history gives way to interpretation, however careful, there must be some risk. I hope, however, that I have in the main let the facts speak for themselves.

The book also keeps within the limited outlook of its original purpose. I need hardly say that not everything which could be said on the subject will be found in it, for such was not my intention. I have tried, more modestly, to map out a path, in some ways a new one, within the restricted sphere of my competence, leaving to others the task of exploring the various complementary aspects of the problem. Having for many years been interested in the institutions of the early church, it is primarily in relation to them that I have approached the particuıar question of marriage and celibacy in the pastoral service of the church.

To avoid giving a false impression, it is perhaps important to make clear, in addition, that I have not set out purely and simply to write another "history of ecclesiastical celibacy." What I have, in fact, been chiefly concerned about, throughout this study, has been the *structures* of the church's pastoral service—and in the structural order there are two services which must concern us specially: the word, and the eucharist. Indeed, it has been these two which have, from the first, most constantly and directly contributed to forming and sustaining the "base community"; and this consideration has governed the essential lines along which my thinking has developed.

It has also determined its sense of proportion. For, in my study, preoccupation with the *styles of life*—especially marriage and celibacy—has always remained subordinate to the—for many reasons, far more important—preoccupation with the actual structures of pastoral service. In fact, marriage and celibacy have only come under study to the extent that both, under the different influences of different structures, both share a common purpose: to serve, to minister to, the hope of the gospel.

This point of view was first forced on me by history. By and large, it may be said that the church's pastoral tradition up to the middle of the fourth century was far more concerned with the services themselves than with the style of life that went with them. But from the point when the old *styles* of life, dictated by convention and custom, began to turn into definite *states* of life with a meaning and value in themselves, which could be idealized and then to that extent subjected to stricter and stricter regulations and laws, the whole pattern of pastoral thinking became profoundly altered.

For from then on it became quite natural that preference should be given to what was thought to be better in itself. It is well known that anything which is thought to be "better in itself" is also all too likely to acquire the awesome aura of immutability. But what, in all this, was to become of that humble attention to the practical—and always more or less changing—needs of that service of the gospel hope which is really the major objective of all pastoral work? The present situation is a living witness to us of what has in fact happened. In the end we can be left with no doubt that history joins its voice to the problems of our own in calling upon us to return to the outlook of the pastoral tradition of the early church, which, from the first, estimated styles of life in relation to pastoral service rather than in themselves.

The old priority of structures and services over styles of life also explains the special attention given to the home and the customs of domestic hospitality in the pastoral theology of the early church, from the apostolic age on. This is a terrain not much explored up to now, and yet it seems to me to contain some of the most lastingly fruitful ideas in the church's pastoral tradition. And it is also in this context of the home—where the assembly used to take place in earliest times —that I have been led to analyze the position given to marriage in the structures of pastoral service in the early church.

Now, as far as pastoral structures are concerned, it was actually the itinerant ministry of the word which first led to a break in the network of family ties. Such breaks, however, which involved first of all those who gave themselves most totally to the service of the gospel, took a variety of forms in the beginning. But in every case, as soon as a person set out to serve the gospel in any way, he must first of all be able to "leave all"—which meant being able to envisage the loosening, if not the breaking, of many bonds, among which for a great many, certainly, the conjugal bond itself would be the chief.

This situation changed fairly rapidly, however. The itinerant service of the word, of which the apostles' work was the prototype, soon yielded most of its original pre-eminence to the permanent service of the assembly which grew out of the welcome given to the gospel message. Ultimately, therefore, it is in the context of the service of the assembly that I have had to consider the problem of the origins of the law of ecclesiastical celibacy. As we know, the first step here was continence within marriage, and as far as the service of the assembly was concerned, it was first patterns of behavior, then customs, and finally regulations relating to married continence, which paved the way for the law of celibacy for clerics in major orders.

It is most noteworthy, however, that the reasons which at the time motivated this last step were drawn in the first place, not from the service of the word, but from the service of the eucharist—though, naturally, there was no lack of reference to the example given in the past by those engaged in the itinerant service of the word in order to promote the new movement. This, in my opinion, is the core of the matter, and it is this point that I have above all set out to show in what follows.

In effect, it seems to me that a single factor was the truly decisive one in the development which gradually turned behavior, customs, and regulations into a *law* in the strictest sense, imposed from above and obligatory for all. This factor ultimately belonged to the age-old and irreducible sense of incompatibility between the impure and the sacred. It became evidently active from the moment when the sacralization of the church's pastoral service had built up in the Christian consciousness energies powerful enough to bring out the latent conflict which already existed in embryo in the feeling that some impurity attached to sexuality as such. Characteristically this moment also coincided with an ever sharper tendency in pastoral thinking to define the church's pastoral service essentially in relation to the sacred, as represented primarily, and immutably, by the *altar* where the eucharist was celebrated; whereas the spontaneous tendency of primitive tradition had been, on the contrary, to define pastoral service above all in relation to the more diverse needs of the *assembly*, as witness, among other things, the "pastoral" imagery itself.

I should like finally to say, that throughout my study, I have made it a point always to refer to a genuine pastoral *tradition*, not merely to things that chanced to happen at one or another time in the dim past of the church. In this, history has been for me only the appropriate instrument for a search whose proper object is something far more than simple historical fact. I have not neglected the importance of that fact: indeed, being accustomed by my profession to this type of observation, I would never make the mistake of bringing back by force into the present what I know that the irreversible march of time has swept away for ever.

But, beyond the brute historical fact, it seems to me that what we have here is the pastoral tradition of the church. Now, if there is such a tradition, and if that tradition remains for us genuinely alive, as it must, then we can only see this: that the tradition, however far we take it into the past, bears upon our own situation, and spreads like a leaven of creation and renewal right up to this age to which we belong, and which is preparing the gospel hope for the generations to come. And this living continuity becomes impressed on us more powerfully than ever when we realize that, in the final analysis, what history links with in the past is none other than one of the essential components of the apostolic tradition itself.

I am aware, of course, how difficult it is to judge of a long, and therefore complex, tradition—to separate what is ephemeral in it from what is permanent, the more or less outworn values from those which remain ever creative. But this difficulty does not seem to dispense one from the obligation to try. It is therefore in this perspective, and this spirit, that I have concluded by considering the problem which seems to me capital, of what I have called the "base community." I have done this with the profound and long-held conviction, that the problem of clerical celibacy is closely tied up with the far wider problem of the actual structures of pastoral service, and most urgently of all, with the particular problem of the structures of pastoral service proper to the "base community."

Let me make myself clear: I in no way underestimate the legitimate anxiety and the ideas of those who think here first and foremost of the "difficulties" arising from celibacy. I have personally seen too many tragedies—inhuman and destructive, as tragedies always are, and unjust and fruitless too—to make that mistake. I believe, however, that it would at the present time be a serious error on our part to see the problem set by the *law* of pastoral celibacy in terms no wider than this. Beyond the personal "difficulties" encountered by a certain number of clergy in the celibate life, there is above all the other, connected problem of the structures of pastoral service of the "base community." And this, in my opinion, is what ultimately governs the other. In other words, unless both problems are resolved together, neither can be truly resolved at all.

I have tried in what I have just said to speak both respectfully and frankly. I am not blind. I am also aware, I think, of all that the church's pastoral services owes to the effectiveness and nobility of the celibate life. But there seems to me at the same time a special pastoral urgency in the situation now. In the long run, there is little use in partial adjustments; we can only be guided by reflecting at depth upon the structures. Such reflection should be conducted with courage and lucidity, and also with the minimum of that excitement which stirs up so much dust that nothing can be seen at all. All I have done here is to put forward some suggestions; but I should be happy if they were to provide a starting point for others who will develop what is worth developing, correct what is incorrect, and simply leave aside what is of no use.

I do think, however, that time presses. For, fundamentally, it is not a question of our posing the problem of celibacy and marriage in the pastoral service of the church, but of the problem's imposing itself upon us. It has arisen largely out of two major phenomena of our time, outside the control of pastoral activity: demographic growth, and the general urbanization of our planet. These two phenomena are growing before our eyes with a force and speed which will not allow us to waste any time; we have at the most a generation in which to find an acceptable solution to the problems I am concerned with here. Any later, and the vastness of the task can only multiply the difficulties to the impossible. The priests who will be in the prime of life around the years 2000 are starting school now. As I have been writing this book, I have been haunted by the thought of them: I should like to dedicate it to them, as a small contribution to that permanent service of the gospel hope of which they will in their turn bear the responsibility.

It also seems to me desirable that considerations on marriage and celibacy in the pastoral ministry of the church should be put forward, not just to the clergy, but to all Christians concerned over the needs and hopes of the present time. We are indissolubly one body, and the awareness of this solidarity, heightened by friendship and by so many common preoccupations, has been the final influence in determining my writing of this book.

I had finished my study some months before the *Decree on the Ministry and Life of Priests (Presbyterorum urdinis)* was adopted by the second Vatican Council, and then officially promulgated at the session of December 7, 1965. The sixteenth paragraph of the decree declares that the practice of "perfect and perpetual continence on behalf of the kingdom of heaven" (Mt 19 : 12), though "not . . . demanded by the very nature of the priesthood, as is evident from the practice of the primitive Church and from the tradition of the Eastern Church," nevertheless "accords with the priesthood on many scores." That practice, recommended by Jesus, and held in high esteem by the universal church, is in fact particularly well adapted to the priest's "mission," which is to consecrate himself wholly to the service of the "new humanity"; with his intention to give himself undividedly to Christ, the better to serve God and men; and, finally, with that twofold witness of charity and hope which his service itself bears among the Christian community. The decree continues:

> For these reasons, which are based on the mystery of the Church and her mission, celibacy was at first recommended to priests. Then, in the Latin Church, it was imposed by law on all who were to be promoted

to sacred orders. This legislation, to the extent that it concerns those who are destined for the priesthood, this most holy Synod again approves and confirms.[1]

I am only too happy to recognize the beauty, the majesty, and—in its own order—the profound justice of that teaching; and I defer to the disciplinary rule which arises out of it. But a council is not a gathering of historians, and consequently it was certainly no part of the purpose of the decree I have just quoted to broach the historical question of the establishment of the law of celibacy for clergy in the pastoral service of the church. Since the council, as before it, those whose special task it is to explore such things thus remain entirely free to pursue their research along the normal lines of documentary criticism. The Christian community will always be best served by such freedom, which is, after all, in theory at least, recognized by everyone. As far as my own work is concerned, therefore, it seems to me to be my duty to present the observations and conclusions which I have for a long time found compelling.

It is important to note, also, that on discussing celibacy in a chapter mainly dealing with "the life of priests" (chapter 3), the conciliar decree made no attempt to face the vast and difficult problem of what I have called "the structures of the base community." This remains a most inadequately explored territory, and a great deal of research on the lines of various different disciplines would certainly be needed for us to get any kind of organic vision of the whole of it. Yet it is, in my opinion, from the standpoint of the "structures of the base community" rather than from that of the "life" of pastors, that the problem of the "law" of clerical celibacy will become more urgently in need of solution in the near future. Since my study has been wholly made from this relatively new point of view, which the conciliar decree could not and did not touch on, it seems to me that this could be a useful moment to put forward briefly here the major results of my observations. I can only hope that this small book will be of some service to the Christian community, and that it may be welcomed with the same hope that has sustained me while writing it.

J.-P. Audet

Jerusalem,
July 1967

[1] W. M. Abbott and J. Gallagher eds., *The Documents of Vatican II*, London 1966, pp. 565–66.

Part One

HOME AND MARRIAGE
IN THE PASTORAL SERVICE OF
THE EARLY CHURCH

1

The Thread of History

The general title of the first part of this study may perhaps cause some surprise; most people, I imagine, would expect me to put celibacy first. But, first of all, if excuse is needed, I would simply point out that the ground has already been explored many times from that starting point; and it is in any case a very limited one. Secondly, I am convinced that all the works produced under that heading, in the Latin church at least, generally suffer to a greater or less extent from one serious, and possibly inevitable, defect. For they presuppose, quite simply, that as institutions, celibacy and pastoral service form the perfect combination. From this it is but a step, very easily made, to the further presupposition that the church was from the first, and totally, tending towards the ideal situation we now have with our law of ecclesiastical celibacy.

The result is that the marriage of the clergy in the early centuries is seen from the first as a kind of left-over "residue" which the early church had inherited—against its own deepest wish—from an earlier, ill-defined situation generally attributable to "human weakness", to the urgent needs of the moment, and to the survival of ideas about the subject which were handed on from Judaism as well as from Greco-Roman paganism, even before the advent of the still more disturbing contribution of the barbarian world. Hence, by the various stages of habit, custom, regulation, and law, the history of clerical celibacy comes to appear simply as a long and glorious "battle" for the gradual elimination of the undesirable "residue" inherited from early days,

3

and at the same time for the establishment of a regime of total continence—sometimes rather ambiguously described as "perfect chastity", since it seems to have been yet another presupposition that this latter can exist only apart from marriage.

It is legitimate to wonder, however, whether such a view of the historical situation does perfect justice to the facts. In any case, some verification of the most commonly accepted presuppositions would certainly be welcome. Furthermore, it does not appear that we have made any great effort up to now to appreciate the positive values that marriage could have represented actually within the pastoral service of the early church. As our analysis develops, we shall have occasion to find in addition how much, and how concretely, the positive values of marriage were linked, in the structures of the pastoral service, with the equally positive values of the "home", which then supplied the most usual and normal context for the two-fold service of the word and of the assembly.

Yet those positive values must have been recognized quite spontaneously and quite clearly, at least by the earliest generations, for there can be no other explanation of the perfect serenity with which those generations seem to have from the first accepted the marriage of deacons, presbyters (priests), and *episcopi* (bishops). It is undoubtedly a problem that requires serious attention from the historians.

Around 190, Polycrates of Ephesus, spokesman for the bishops of Asia in the Easter controversy, wrote a defensive letter to Pope Victor and the church of Rome, of which Eusebius reproduced a part. Among other things, Polycrates urges the traditions of his own family (*suggeneis*). At sixty-five, he was eighth in an episcopal line and thus, he considered, able to date his liturgical traditions back to the turn of the second century. He even seems to want to make it quite clear, *en passant*, that he was descended in direct line from several of the bishops he is successor to (*hois kai parekolouthesa tisin auton*). And all this, he says to Rome, not merely without any trace of embarrassment, but actually with the proudest sense of there being, in this situation, a most important factor of continuity and stability for the great church of Ephesus.[1]

At the end of the second century, the state of things in this respect cannot have been very different in Rome from what it was in Ephesus,

---

[1] Eusebius, *Historia ecclesiastica* v, 24, 6–7.

and probably in all the churches of Asia Minor. Thirty years later, we learn by chance from the author of the *Philosophumena*, that Pope Callixtus (217-22) made no apology for leaving clergy who got married to continue in their position.[2] Hippolytus, as we know, was here settling an òld score: he castigated the pope's conduct in no uncertain terms, even making it seem to have been a scandalous innovation. Yet it is quite clear that Callixtus would have found it difficult to act as he did had he not in fact had the support of the general opinion of the Roman community, as well as of the accepted customs in his church's tradition.

A similar situation seems to have prevailed at that time in Carthage and Alexandria. Tertullian certainly knew a certain number of unmarried clerics. "How many men," he cried, "and how many women, in the [various] orders of the church, in the name of continence, have preferred to marry only God . . . !"[3] *Quanti igitur et quantae!* His phrase has often been taken, at least tacitly, as meaning a reference to multitudes, thereby apparently becoming suitable as a basis for a more general interpretation according to which the majority of the clergy of the time were already living in celibacy.

But neither this interpretation of the phrase, nor of the total situation, seem to be justified by the wording Tertullian actually uses. The question is one of the language, and of his style: in oratorical Latin, *quantus* can mean larger or smaller numbers depending on the situation: a certain number, even a large number perhaps, but it does not normally indicate a majority, and still less a near totality, of the people or things under consideration. "If a sharing of names can do injury to anyone," wrote Tertullian again, elsewhere, "how many bad slaves (*quanti nequam servi*) are harming the names of the kings Alexander, Darius, and Holophernes!"[4] It would be clearly absurd to claim this as proving that the majority of bad slaves in Tertullian's neighbourhood were named Alexander, Darius, and Holophernes, or, conversely, that the majority of slaves named Alexander, Darius, and Holophernes were bad. All we need say, to make sense of the phrase, is that it was not unusual at that time to find unsatisfactory slaves decked out in those illustrious names.

And there is nothing to suggest that we must depart from this

[2] Hippolytus, *Philosophumena* IX, 12, 22.
[3] Tertullian, *De exhortatione castitatis* XIII, 4.
[4] Tertullian, *Adversus Marcionem* I, 7, 2; and, in the same sense, *De anima*, 46, 10.

natural use of *quantus* when the same author writes: "How many men and how many women, in the [various] orders of the church, in the name of continence, have preferred to marry only God . . . !" The obvious meaning is that examples of celibacy among the clergy are not unusual—that there are a certain number, and possibly a fairly large number. But it would certainly be twisting the sense of the text to see *quanti* as a majority, still more the great majority, of the clergy engaged in pastoral service.

This interpretation seems to me to be implicitly confirmed, further, elsewhere, by Tertullian himself. In *De exhortatione castitatis*, Tertullian tries to persuade his friend, and reader, not to remarry. He urges, among other reasons, the somewhat delicate situation which, it seems to him, the remarriage could not fail to create in regard to prayer and the eucharist.

> Are you then going to present yourself before the Lord with as many wives as you can recall in prayer? Will you also make the oblation for them both, and recommend them both through the intercession of a bishop who has come forward from one marriage only, or even from virginity (*aut etiam de virginitate*) to ordination and to sanctification?[5]

The *aut etiam* here would seem to make it necessary for us to see this as an allusion to the situation of the once-married bishop as being the most usual one, and that of the celibate bishop as the exception—even though, clearly, Tertullian himself considers the latter to be by far the more desirable in itself.

We know, however, thanks to the deacon Pontius, that Caecilius, the priest who brought Cyprian to the Christian faith, was married, and that it was to him, whose friendship and veneration he soon gained, that Caecilius before dying bequeathed the care of his wife and children.[6] Cyprian's personal correspondence, it is true, makes mention of only one married priest, the unfortunate Novatus.[7] But we

[5] Tertullian, *De exhortatione castitatis* xi, 2. I here translate *sacerdos* as bishop, which seems demanded by Tertullian's normal use of it. But that use is not as rigid as has been claimed in the past. There are places where one may hesitate— among others, where he explicitly extends to the whole "sacerdotal order," including priests (*presbyteri*), the rule of "monogamy" to which the bishop (*summus sacerdos*) is first of all subject. (*De exhortatione castitatis* vii, 2 and 6. See also *De baptismo* xvii, 1; and compare *Apologeticum* xxxix, 5; *De corona* iii, 3.)

[6] *Vita Cypriani*, 4 (ed. Hartel iii, 2, xciv–xcv).

[7] Cyprian, *Letters* iii, 2, 5. We may also see the letter of Caledonius, in which there is mentioned a certain Felix (xxiv, 1), who "assisted" the *presbyterium* in

must not conclude from Cyprian's habitual silence on the question of married clergy that in the middle of the third century married priests were only a rare exception in the African church. Such a conclusion would certainly be false, for the general situation in this regard cannot in fact have changed much since Tertullian's time. Indeed, the argument could be very easily turned the other way—for Cyprian is equally silent about continence and clerical celibacy.[8] We can only conclude, in fact, that to all appearances the situation remained undisturbed, as it had been for generations.

Nor have we any very precise information about Egypt. But the serene liberty and breadth of vision with which Clement of Alexandria expressed himself made it clear that he, at least, was not concerned with exceptional situations. Having quoted 1 Tim 5 : 14–15, in which Paul recommends young widows to remarry, he continues, adopting Paul's views: "Of course, [the apostle] also wholly admits [*panu apodechetai*]"—and how can we fail to admit also?—"that the husband of one wife", be he priest,[9] deacon, or layman, if he uses marriage without reproach, "will be saved through bearing children" (1 Tim 2 : 15).[10]

Upon a careful reading in their proper literary context, the texts of Origen which are so often quoted do not, I think, suggest anything different. Origen distinguishes between the priestly "function" and the "merit" of him who fills it, and he notes that it is easy to find someone to take up the "function", but on the other hand there are few (*pauci*) whom we find "adorned" with all the virtues needed to carry it out. It is in this context that he states that he personally (*sed ego*) would not

---

some way, and was married. Felix and his wife Victoria, having once offered sacrifice, were exiled and had their possessions confiscated for remaining true to the faith later on after a renewal of persecution. It has been suggested that Felix was a deacon (*presbyterium subministrabat*), but this remains only a hypothesis.

[8] A passing allusion to Pope Cornelius LV, 8, 3; see also *De habitu virginum*, 4.

[9] *Presbuteros* here may well mean, in the wider sense, a member of the "presbyteral" college, which would include first and foremost the bishop presiding over it.

[10] Clement of Alexandria, *Stromata* III, 12, 90, 1; see also III, 18, 108, 2. As is generally the case, we only find chance scraps of information about individual cases. Of Cheremon, for instance, bishop of Nilopolis, who was forced to flee with his wife to the Arabian mountains, where it seemed that they both soon died; and Phileas, bishop of Thmuis, previously an important and rich functionary, and married to an unbelieving wife, who was martyred in Alexandria under Maximinius. (Eusebius, *Historica ecclesiastica* VI, 42, 3, which refers to Denys of Alexandria; and VIII, 9, 7–8; also, for Phileas, Ruinart, *Acta primorum martyrum sincera et selecta: Acta sanctorum Phileas et Phileromi martyrum*, 1–2, 548–50.)

be willing to extend to the "priests of the church" the rule of the Levitical priesthood which required priests to provide for their own succession by having children. This, he considered, was a situation not always free from a certain "indulgence" in matters of chastity— an "indulgence" Origen was unwilling to facilitate. Among us, he continues, things appear in a different light, for if in the church priests and doctors can generate children, it is after the fashion of him who said: "My little children, with whom I am again in travail, until Christ be formed in you" (Gal 4 : 19).[11] As far as we can tell, this was put forward by Origen as the expression of an ideal, and not a statement of fact on the customs then in force in the church of his day.

For Syria, we need not enlarge on the evidence of the *Didascalia* (from the latter half of the third century) which is perfectly clear, and which notably takes it for granted that marriage is part of the normal situation of the service of the episcopate:

> It is required that the bishop be thus: a man that hath taken one wife, that hath governed his house well. And thus let him be proved when he receives the imposition of hands to sit in the office of the bishopric: whether he be chaste, and whether his wife also be a believer and chaste; and whether he has brought up his children in the fear of God, and admonished and taught them; and whether his household fear and reverence him, and all of them obey him. For if his household in the flesh withstand him and obey him not, how shall they that are without his house become his, and be subject to him?[12]

By and large, up to the last decades of the third century, therefore, it was marriage rather than continence or celibacy as a style of life which seems to have been the *dominant reality* virtually everywhere in the pastoral service of the church. This is the situation we must begin

[11] Origen, *Homilies on Leviticus* VI, 6.

[12] *Didascalia Apostolorum*, trans. and ed. R. Hugh Connolly, Oxford 1929, 32. In all this there remain certain concrete facts which we must not lose sight of. The *Didascalia* requires that, except in special circumstances, the bishop be at least fifty. This rule almost certainly reflects customs which were both ancient and widespread in the church. Since, on the other hand, at this time, the various functions of the pastoral service were far more "open" than they later became, it is clear that a number of bishops, priests, and even deacons were taking up their respective charges at a time in their lives when their decision to marry had been made long before. The marriage of the clergy was therefore in the first place a situation of fact. A parallel, though reverse, situation came about later, when it became more and more usual to lay hands upon celibates and monks whose original decision was not made with a view to pastoral service at all.

from. Whatever may have been said by others, history as a whole does not seem to me to be open to any other interpretation.

In fact, outside gnostic, encratite, or montanist circles, all of which were shot through with the dualism endemic in the world outside the church, it was only at the beginning of the third century that the first, still sporadic, signs of a certain tension between marriage and celibacy for the clergy begin to appear in our documents—and, in particular, in Tertullian, who was in fact, some time around the years 208-9, to turn openly to montanism. If we follow out a comparison of certain themes, and also certain insistent references to examples from the past, adapted to suit the tastes of the day, we sense a profound transformation gradually taking place in people's minds. At the same time, a similar ferment can also be found about the marriage of the faithful. A whole literature was taking shape whose distinctive features were enthusiastic praise of virginity, exhortations to a certain style of "chastity", and impassioned discussion of the merits of widowhood. In addition, this literature was, from many points of view, definitely a fighting weapon.

In this general atmosphere the first shots were fired in the "battle" for the "perfect chastity" of the clergy. Further, as I shall try to explain later on (part 2, chapter 5), it was no mere chance that this "battle" should have coincided in time with the appearance in Christian vocabulary of the first signs of a process of sacralization of the pastoral service of the church. It was really only to be expected that the recognition of the sacred would then begin to draw the "pure" into its orbit; and in the eyes of many people, the "pure" here referred above all to the names of all forms of sexual abstinence: *virginity, continence* and *widowhood*. It all hung together.

At the dawn of the fourth century, the Council of Elvira laid down the first law on the point recorded in history. This first ruling referred not to celibacy, in the narrow sense the term was later to be given, but to the style of married life for clergy already married: bishops, priests, deacons, in short without exception "all the clergy engaged in the ministry" (*omnibus clericis positis in ministerio*). These married clergy were ordered by the Spanish council to "abstain" henceforth "from their wives" (*abstinere se a coniugibus suis*), and no longer seek to have children (*et non generare filios*). Though such a ban may seem to us to have created a somewhat confused situation, at least the punishment had the merit of being simple and clear: anyone who disobeyed was to be deprived of his functions.[13]

In the fourth century itself, and those which followed, the West was to see a long series of regulations similar to the one I have mentioned, until the first and second councils of the Lateran (1123 and 1139) finally took the ultimate step of declaring the nullity, or annulment, of any marriage of a cleric in major orders.[14] In fact, however, this decision did little more than carry to its logical conclusion the labors of Leo IX and his successors from the middle of the previous century onwards. Thus it is only from the eleventh and twelfth centuries that one can properly speak of a "law of ecclesiastical celibacy" for the Latin church as a whole.

It is important, again, to note that the ruling of the Lateran was made in a climate of claims, repressions, and sanctions unknown in the days of the earlier rules, at least in that form and with that degree of tension. Indeed, the marriage of priests—the "heresy of the nicolites," as it came to be called in the second half of the eleventh century—was by now not far from appearing as an unmitigated evil to be extirpated at all costs. Contrary to the old rules—or to what we imagine them to have been, since we do not know exactly—and certainly without any assimilation of their spirit, the state of married

---

[13] Canon 33 (Denzinger-Schönmetzer, 119). According to Socrate, *Histoire ecclésiastique* I, 11, "the bishops" present at the Council of Nicaea in 325 intended at one moment to legislate in the same terms, but a heartfelt and vigorous intervention from the Egyptian Paphnutius dissuaded them from doing so.

As regards the situation of the wives resulting from canon 33 of Elvira, see canon 27 (Denzinger-Schönmetzer, 118), in which all clergy, *episcopus vel quilibet alius clericus*, were forbidden to keep with them (presumably in the dwellings attached to the *ecclesia*) any women other than their own sisters or daughters, and these only on the express condition that they had vowed their virginity to God (*virginem dicatam Deo*). One may wonder whether, by implication, the council's real intention was to remove the wives themselves from the priests' houses. Compare this with the more trusting and moderate—as well as more realistic—solution of Pope Leo the Great in the fifth century: "The law of continence (*lex continentiae*) is the same for ministers of the altar (*ministris altaris*) as for bishops and priests. As long as these were laymen, or lectors, they could rightfully contract marriage and have children. But from the moment of their entering the aforementioned positions, what had been legitimate for them began to be so no longer. From then on, turning a carnal union into a spiritual marriage, they must, though not sending away their wives, have them as though not having them, in such a way that the charity of the spouses be preserved, and that the exercise of the conjugal right at the same time cease" (Letter to Rusticus of Narbonne, 3 [PL 54, 1204]).

[14] See canons 7 (Denzinger-Schönmetzer, 711) and 21 of Lateran I, and canon 7 of Lateran II (Hefele-Leclercq, *Histoire des conciles* V–1, 633, 638, and 726f.

priests came to be looked upon by most of the great promoters of reform as purely and simply the fruit of vice. For that reason, the marriage of priests could deserve only condemnation and punishment: the close and constant association of simony and nicolaism in the writings of the reformers of the time is enough in itself to indicate what illogicalities resulted from this in pastoral thinking.

On both sides, the "battle"—and now it really was a battle!—was fought with the methods and in the fashion of the time, which was rugged and extremist, as quick to violence as to tears of devotion and repentance. In some places the juridical and social mechanism of feudalism and serfdom were put at the service of the cause. In order to isolate those who resisted, the faithful were forbidden to take part in services celebrated by pastors with wives or concubines.[15]

Now, so many years later, we find it easy enough in our theology to explain, and reiterate, that the celibacy of the clergy is a "lofty expediency" of their "ministry", and no more. But history cannot conceal from itself the fact that this "lofty expediency" as given the force of a "law" under the patronage of a conception of the pastoral ministry whose methods and ways of action can suggest only one thing: inflexible necessity which none can escape.

Compared with the injunctions and demands of the eleventh- and twelfth-century councils, canon 33 of the Council of Elvira, though already expressed with considerable rigidity, seems a monument of light and peace. It may be said to stand, spiritually, halfway between the apostolic age and its extension into the second century, and the stormy reforms of the Middle Ages. It might, therefore, help to clarify matters if we examine together with it certain complementary observations, noting, as the occasion arises, the major later developments.

The ruling made by Elvira presupposes two situations accepted both in people's minds and in fact. The first was voluntary continence: this was the basis of the rule. It had on its side, if not the majority of the clergy—from what we can judge—at least the weight of prestige. It embodied a spiritual ideal which the whole community united in recognizing. However, this ideal of voluntary continence, as we shall see, did not then appear to be of its nature linked with pastoral service, for it was in fact shared not only by a number of

---

[15] Lateran Council, April 1059; and Council of Rome, March 1074. The ban was reiterated on several occasions in the years that followed.

clergy, but also, on the female side, by the virgins and widows, and on the male side, by the ascetics. It was thus by way of extension that the ideal of continence came to be connected with the style of life of the clergy involved in the pastoral "ministry". Far from starting there, it was on the contrary the community itself which came to put the two together.

The second situation involved was, of course, that of marriage. As we have seen, the council required on this point that bishops, priests, and deacons should "abstain from their wives" from the moment of entering upon the functions belonging to their "ministry", under pain of being removed from office (*ab honore clericatus exterminetur*). What is of special interest to us here is the motive which inspired the rule, and on this the council does not enlarge; presumably there was no need. It was something well known, requiring only a slight allusion to make it clearly understood by everyone.

On analyzing it, however, it is clear once that there was no intention of setting the bishop, priest, or deacon who was married free of his family cares. Nor was the purpose, at least primarily, to make clerics in major orders more available for the service of their church. Though obliged to continence, they remained in effect normally responsible for supporting and directing their households. From this point of view, the obligation to continence in no way made the circumstances of married clergy any easier: it might indeed make it even more burdensome (see canon 27, cited above).

Furthermore, canon 19 gives us a passing glimpse of one particular case in which bishops, priests, and deacons continued to be personally responsible for the running of their own affairs: the case of trade. Here, to avoid overlengthy absences, the council demanded that bishops, priests, and deacons who were engaged in business should not leave their "province" for the purpose of trying to find more lucrative business deals elsewhere. If they had business to settle outside the "province," they must send if possible one of their sons, or a freeman, or a servant, or a friend, or someone else. This example makes it very clear that at the time, and in Spain, the rule of married continence for clerics in major orders by no means involved any abandonment of their professional or domestic responsibilities.

The true motive underlying the council's ruling must therefore be sought elsewhere. In effect, the motive is more or less made clear in the text itself, for we find it in a single word mentioned casually in an explanatory clause: *ministerium*. This is the key word. In Christian

Latin of the period, when referring to pastoral service, the *ministerium* was in fact generally seen as a *sacrum ministerium*.[16] Now it was certainly not primarily, nor chiefly, for the part they took within the "liturgy" in a "service of the word" that the respective functions of bishop, priest, and deacon were seen as a *ministerium* (*sacrum*). At the beginning of the fourth century the lector also had a regular and well-recognized function in the "service of the word," and yet he was never counted among those who were strictly speaking engaged in the "ministry"; nor, therefore, did anyone think of subjecting him to the rule of married continence when he was of an age to have a wife and children.[17]

What constituted the Christian *ministerium* was thus actually the service of the *sacramenta* properly so called, especially, of course, the service of the supreme *sacramentum*, the eucharist. Ultimately, therefore, it was the direct service of the eucharist, seen as *sacramentum*, which determined the rule of married continence for the married bishop, priest, and deacon from the moment of entering on the functions of their respective "ministries."

It seems to me quite clear from this that it was a perception of the "sacred" which underlay the notion of sexual abstinence even within marriage. And from this it becomes equally clear that the rule of married continence for clergy involved in the direct service of the *sacramenta*[18] rested in turn upon another perception that was already firmly established in people's minds: that which, distinguishing between the "pure" and the "impure," classed the exercise of sexuality in any form among those things which must be kept apart from the *sacra*.[19]

There seems no other possible explanation as to how so strict an obligation of conscience could have been introduced in the Christian

[16] Compare the Greek *leitourgia* and *hierourgia* at the same period.

[17] In Hippolytus' *Apostolic tradition*, the lector enters upon his function by simply being given the book of lessons: the bishop did not lay hands on him (ed. Dix, 12, 21).

[18] "Qui sacramentis divinis inserviunt," Council of Carthage, June 16, 390, canon 2; compare for this latter formula, and also the general tendency of thought, Cyprian, *Letters* LXXII, 2: "It is necessary, indeed, that the priests and ministers who serve the altar and the sacrifices (*sacerdotes et ministros qui altari et sacrificiis deserviunt*) be without spot or stain, according to the word of the Lord God, who has said in Leviticus: 'No man . . . who has a blemish shall come near to offer the Lord's offerings.' "

[19] In Christian language they were called *sacramenta*, probably to avoid using the word *sacra* with all its connections with pagan worship.

world, even within legitimate marriage, for clergy called to the direct service of the *sacramenta*. For what the ruling of Elvira was in fact dealing with was not marriage as such, since there was no question of abandoning that either at the time or in the future, even for the clergy of the *ministerium*, but simply and solely the exercise of sexuality within marriage.

For this to be so, it must first have been thought that there was something irremediably unfitting in the ultimate encounter of the exercise of sexuality with the service of the *sacramenta*. How else can we possibly understand? In no other way, it seems to me: we are here confronted with an interplay of relationships between the "pure" and the "sacred." The latter, with the primacy normally accorded to it in the order of values, attracts the former, but excludes even the possibility of contact with the "impure," which is its opposite.[20]

As is well known, there is nothing specifically Christian about the value-structure which works out fitting distances between the "impure" and the "sacred." On the contrary, it goes back to the oldest religious roots of mankind, and is to be found at all times and in all places. The question is: When did this value structure enter and become implanted in our pastoral tradition? We can trace its path through the third century with a fair degree of ease, but it is harder to recognize it in the second. The further back in time the historian goes, the more he finds himself faced with a problem of continuity.

We must, therefore, go right back and examine our Christian origins, see what the position was at the very beginning. Thus we must consider first and foremost the behavior and thinking of Jesus himself.

---

[20] It is significant that the third-century *Didascalia* thought it necessary to argue vigorously against an idea of sexual "impurity" similar in every way to that which seems to underlie canon 33 of Elvira. (See especially vi, 21–2; Connolly, 242–54.) Compare also with the Elvira ruling canon 44 of the Council of Laodicea (mid-fourth century), which rules "that women"—simply on the ground of their femininity!—"must not enter the sanctuary (*thusiasterion*) [or] approach the altar" (Hefele-Leclerq i, 2, 1020).

2

The Behavior and Thinking of Jesus

From our standpoint, it is useful to begin by pointing out that at no point does Jesus seem to have wanted to integrate his activities into the sacral apparatus of the Palestinian Judaism of his age.

Here his statements are in marked contrast to those of John the Baptist. For John "preached a *baptism*" (Mk 1 : 4, and parallels), and this type of "baptizing" activity in the son of the priest Zechariah was actually so fully recognized by his contemporaries that the title of "baptist" or "baptizer" seems to have been given him very early on.[1] Thus a most characteristic style of activity made it clear to public opinion what kind of person he was. In early Christian tradition, too, memories of John the Baptist remained chiefly linked with the Jordan and the land around it: the desert, Bethany "beyond the Jordan," and Aenon, "near Salim."

In comparison, though we cannot press the phrase too far, we may say that Jesus' activity was more purely and of set purpose "the word." Certainly, Jesus himself often took that "word" right into the synagogue assemblies and the temple precincts. But any association with the prevailing framework of wordship and the sacred which resulted from his doing so always remained, with him, a chance one, and ultimately of secondary importance. Jesus' "word" seemed just as much at home when it was heard in a meeting house, on the shore of

[1] Mk 6 : 25; Mt 3 : 1; Lk 7 : 20; etc. (*Ioannes ho baptistes*); Mk 1 : 4, etc. (*Ioannes ho baptizon*).

the lake of Tiberias, on the hillsides of Galilee, in the streets and public squares, in the fields, along the wayside, or by Jacob's well. Because it was everything in itself, it could be at ease in every place and circumstance. It could also move equally freely in most of the literary forms then flourishing around it. Largely independent of cult and rite, the "word" of Jesus—partly for that very reason—enjoyed from the first a flexibility and mobility which John's activity never seems to have achieved.[2]

All this may well be obvious; but these are things we often forget, though their value is by no means only a transitory one belonging just to the past. In any case, we must keep them in mind when we are trying to picture to ourselves the original style of activity that was Christ's. What, then, was it like?

As we have said, Jesus' activity was first and foremost wholly "word." Taken as a whole, that "word" took two principal forms: it was a message (*kerugma*), and it was instruction (*didakhè*). And we must note further that the different forms of the "word"—"message" and "instruction"—here resulted in two proportionately distinct styles of life: that of "prophet" (*prophetes*) on the one hand, and of "master" (*didaskalos*) on the other. What I would like to do, therefore, is to examine these facts in relation to others, so as in some ways to simplify our final picture in the interests of clarity and brevity.

The gospel tradition made no pretence to any precise exactitude in either topography or chronology. What it gives us is rather a general picture, and certain guiding marks as to detail which are sometimes hard to reconcile with one another. It seems, however, that the account in Mark contains the most accurate memories of the beginnings of Jesus' activity.

> After John was arrested, Jesus came into Galilee, preaching the gospel of God, and saying, "The time is fulfilled, and the kingdom of God is at hand; repent, and believe in the gospel." [Mk 1 : 14–15.]

---

[2] See St. Paul: "Christ did not send me to baptize, but to preach the gospel (*euaggelizesthai*)" (1 Cor 1 : 17); and again, about Jesus himself, see Jn 4 : 2: "although Jesus himself did not baptize, but only his disciples," which seems to give a more precise version of the more vague phrase in 3 : 22. In effect, it was only later, after Jesus' resurrection, that the new baptism "with the Holy Spirit" (Mk 1 : 8; Jn 1 : 33; etc.) came to have a regular place in the service of the "word" (Acts 2 : 38; Mk 16 : 16; Mt 28 : 19; etc.

This—"the time is fulfilled," etc.—is obviously not a "discourse," nor is it the theme or summing up of a longer "discourse." It is, in the strictest sense, and probably almost in those exact words, the original *message* (*kerugma*) of Jesus. As the writer himself says, it is a "good news" (*euaggelion*), a *gospel* in the original sense.

This, then, was the first object of Jesus' activity. Now, a moment's thought makes it clear that a message of this kind, presented in so compact a form, could only become effective by being made known to a great many people as soon as possible. In other words, to get through, such a message must be continually repeated—not of course to the same audience, but over a wide territory.

And in effect, if one reads it carefully, Mark's account suggests precisely this. It makes it clear that the field of action was Galilee. The style of activity, furthermore, was that of the "herald" of old (*kerusson*), the bearer of messages and news, a widely accepted and very familiar figure. But since here we are concerned with "good news" from God (*euaggelion tou theou*, a genitive of provenance), intended not for a particular individual, but for the whole people for whom "the time" is said to be "fulfilled," it is clear that Jesus wanted from the first to transmit his message quickly to the greatest possible number of hearers. In Mark's account this is underlined by the tenses used for the verbs: "Jesus came into Galilee" (aorist, *elthen*, drawing attention to a point in the past), there "preaching the gospel of God" (*kerusson*, a present-participial construction indicating a continuative action carried on from a definite point in the past).[3]

If my analysis is correct, then what we must see at the beginning of Jesus' public life is a period of indeterminate length, but with its own well-defined character, when Jesus modelled his "word" upon that of the ancient heralds, or—more precisely, perhaps—of the ancient prophets who presented themselves as Yahweh's heralds to his people.

In this connection, the reference to Is 61 : 1-2, in the episode of the reading in the synagogue as recounted in Luke, seems particularly significant:

The Spirit of the Lord is upon me, because he has anointed me to preach good news to the poor. He has sent me to proclaim release to

---

[3] See, in the same sense, but with less clarity in its general line, Mt 4 : 17, 23–5; the version in Lk 4 : 14 remains wholly implicit, and can only be understood in the light of Mark's account.

the captives, and recovering of sight to the blind, to set at liberty those who are oppressed, to proclaim the acceptable year of the Lord.[4]

The gospel tradition does not expand this point, for at that time and in those surroundings, there was no need to do so. But from our standpoint, it is most important to be explicit: it is clear that for Jesus to adopt for his "word," from the beginning, the form of a "message," meant at the same time adopting not only a certain style of behaviour but even a certain style of life.

Now at that time the person of the herald had two characteristics symbolizing at once the function and the type of existence proper to that function; the "voice," and the "feet."[5] The herald is a "voice" in the service of him who has sent him; that is the essence of his function. But he is also a pair of "feet," active, available, free, ready to take the message everywhere; and that is more especially the style of life proper to, and inseparable from, the function. The herald is mobile, for that is his existence. At any moment, he must be ready to leave all things: home, father, mother, brothers, sisters, wife, children, to carry out his mission. Nothing by the wayside must hold him back, nor must there be anything to burden him until he has completed his "course."[6] Another symbol we find here of the function and its accompanying style of life is simplicity of costume (Eph 4 : 15): a certain self-denial is the normal condition of life for a herald.

Thus it is along these lines that we can best picture the beginnings of Jesus' activity in Galilee. In the Near and Far East, as in classical Greece and Rome, the function of the herald had a recognized place in

---

[4] Lk 4 : 18–19. Note that Luke, unlike Mk 6 : 1–6 and Mt 13 : 53–8, places this episode at the beginnings of Jesus' activity; in the narrator's mind, the reading of Is 61 : 1–2 in the Nazareth synagogue clearly took on an exemplary—though polyvalent—value.

[5] Is 40 : 3; "A voice cries: 'In the wilderness prepare. . . .' "; Is 52 : 7: "How beautiful upon the mountains are the feet of him who brings good tidings, who publishes peace, who brings good tidings of good, who publishes salvation, who says to Zion, 'Your God reigns.' " This is quoted in part in Rom 10 : 15; note, too, the explicit reminder of the symbol in Eph 6 : 15; "Having shod your feet with the equipment of the gospel of peace."

[6] Compare St. Paul's words (Acts 20 : 24): "But I do not account my life of any value, nor as precious to myself, if only I may accomplish my course (*ton dromon mou*) and the ministry [*ten diakonian*, literally 'the service'] which I received from the Lord Jesus to testify to the gospel (*to euaggelion*) of the grace [*kharis*, literally 'goodwill,' 'favour,' 'love'] of God"; and also (Acts 13 : 25): "And as John was finishing his course (*ton dromon*) . . . ," where Paul is recorded as representing John as a messenger and herald. See also 2 Tim 4 : 7: "I have fought the good fight, I have finished the race (*ton dromon*)."

the public consciousness and in custom. It was a service that bore the same relationship to ancient society as newspapers, radio, and television bear to ours. For many centuries it was one of the essential organs of social communication at all levels. In Israel, when the prophets, especially those of the great Isaiahan tradition, adopted the social persona of the herald in order to give concrete expression to their relationship with Yahweh on the one hand, and the people on the other, they were doing no more than basing themselves on a sociological prototype long recognized in their world. The function also had a certain prestige: it was certainly not in the interests of Yahweh's heralds to do anything that would mar that image: on the contrary, there was a definite advantage in preserving as much of it as was compatible with the transposition of the prototype into the sphere of religious activity.

Everything suggests that Jesus himself did exactly the same when the time came for him to carry out his mission. In modelling his first work on that of the prophets who were Yahweh's heralds, he was by that very fact modelling it indirectly upon that of the herald of old, whose image may indeed have been very much alive in his mind, quite independent of the prophetic model.[7]

Thus Jesus' first activity in Galilee deliberately took the form of a *message*. That message was not a discourse: it was a concise phrase, a single stunning formula, intended to be repeated as it stood on every possible occasion. The purpose of that shock-phrase seems to have been to make a kind of first crack in the people's hope, through which the whole of God's plan could enter in the future. Certainly the message by itself could not do everything: its purpose was simply to make a beginning. Other means would come in time to carry forward the fulfilment of God's plan, until it should be complete (Jn 17 : 1–26; 19 : 30). But by the very form in which it was expressed, the message had the enormous value of making it possible to affect great numbers from the first. In addition, the brevity and force of the message were supported by the mobility and detachment of the herald. Nothing could hold him back. In a few weeks, perhaps, or more probably in a few months, Jesus seems to have "gone about" preaching in "all Galilee" (Mt 4 : 23). And his "fame" spread even further afield (Mt 4 : 24; Lk 4 : 14).

---

[7] Compare the earlier example of John, to whom early Christian tradition always attached the word-for-word quotation of Is 40 : 3–5: "A voice crying in the wilderness . . ."

But what kind of "fame" could in fact result from this style of activity other than that of a new "prophet?" Jesus' message, and the "signs" that went with it, seemed to most people to give evidence that "the times" of the great hope foretold by the prophets of old "were fulfilled."[8] The continuity was evident: a "prophet" was with them.[9]

I realize that this intention involves a certain conjecture, as indeed any interpretation must. But the area of conjecture is not very great, and certainly not sufficient to cast doubt on our picture as a whole from the very outset. Further, my observations are given solid confirmation from another direction—for would not the first sending of the Twelve have been planned by Jesus along the lines of his own first activity in Galilee, as it appears in my analysis? Of many hypotheses, this seems inherently the most likely.

Certainly, the facts here are exactly what we would expect. The first sending of the Twelve (Mk 6 : 6–13, and parallels) is primarily to give a "message" rather than an "instruction." The Twelve are to "preach" (*ekeruxan*) (Mk 6 : 12); to "preach (*kerussete*) as you go, saying, 'The kingdom of heaven is at hand'" (Mt 10 : 7). Jesus "sent them out to preach (*kerussein*) the kingdom of God" (Lk 9 : 2, 6). The first "message" of the Twelve, then, like that of Jesus, belonged to the style of speaking and acting which characterized the heralds of the past: brief words and rapid movement, both adapted to covering a large area as quickly as possible.

They also had a "mission" in the strictest sense. The herald was "sent," and it was as one sent that he carried out his function (*diakonia*). The Twelve were thus also "sent,"[10] and for them too it was precisely as "men sent" that they were given among the disciples (*mathetai*) the special title of apostles (*apostoloi*) whose function was the direct service of the "good news" (Lk 9 : 6). They were those "sent" by Jesus, just as he knew himself to be "sent" by the Father.[11] The first sending of the Twelve also stresses in retrospect the link between the "signs" and the initial "message" of Jesus in Galilee. In Luke's account, Jesus "sends" the Twelve, not only "to preach the kingdom of God," but also "to heal" (Lk 9 : 2). On this

---

[8] For this interpretation, compare Acts 2 : 16–35: the apostolic "message."

[9] See in particular Lk 4 : 24, which may be a reference, at least in the narrator's intention, to the inaugural period.

[10] *apostellein* (Mk 6 : 7; Mt 10 : 5; Lk 9 : 2; see also Is 6 : 8; 6 : 54–8: 16; 61 : 1; Rom 10 : 15).

[11] This is the general sense of Jesus' baptism in the Jordan; note specially Lk 4 : 14: "And Jesus returned in the power of the Spirit into Galilee."

occasion, all the accounts emphasize the fact that the apostles received from him "power and authority" for that purpose (Lk 9 : 1; Mk 6 : 7, 13; Mt 10 : 8).

In the Palestinian Judaism of the time, to make such an association between the "message" and the "power" to work "signs" could not fail to suggest but one kind of person (at least, to those disposed to recognize the authenticity of the sending): a *prophet* (see Lk 24 : 19). As I have already mentioned in passing, it was above all by the combined effect of his message and the signs that went with it that Jesus himself was first recognized as a prophet. Indeed there may well have been an allusion to that prophetic aspect of the first mission of the Twelve in the saying recorded by Matthew on that occasion: "He who receives a prophet because he is a prophet shall receive a prophet's reward" (10 : 41; see also 5 : 12).

Finally, at the same time as entrusting his "message" to them, Jesus gave the Twelve a certain number of recommendations as to how they should carry out their mission, and the style of life they should adopt for the journey. They were to go from town to town, from village to village, and from house to house. Thus it was "as they went" (*poreuomenoi*, Mt 10 : 7) that they were to "preach" the good news that the "kingdom of heaven" had come. They were to be mobile, as a herald must be, and for the same reason, they were to maintain their freedom, not letting themselves be held up either by the good or by the bad reception they might get. They were to live on the hospitality offered them, just as it came, provided only it be "worthy" (Mt 10 : 11). For their clothing and other necessities, they were to take only the absolute minimum. In this way nothing would delay them on their journey: they were to be detached, they were to be free. They could present to everyone the image of the true herald of God, the bearer of the "good news" of hope, as Jesus himself had no doubt shown them how, in the beginnings of his activity in Galilee. For in this case the "master" would not have to recommend to his "disciples" a style of life much different from the one he had himself adopted in similar circumstances.[12]

Thus, it is possible for us to get in retrospect a fairly precise idea of Jesus' earliest activity in Galilee from the first sending of the Twelve. In essence, he was presenting himself then as a "prophet," a herald of Yahweh, "mighty in deed and word" (Lk 24 : 19). From town to

---

[12] Compare the sending of the seventy or the seventy-two disciples in Lk 10 : 1–16, which provides evidence in support of this.

town, from village to village, from house to house, from synagogue to synagogue, he spread his message: "The time is fulfilled, and the kingdom of God is at hand; repent, and believe in [this] gospel" (Mk 1 : 15). It was done quickly, in order to create a first shock of hope.

Introduced in this way into the minds of chance hearers, however, the message had a very limited scope, as Jesus himself must more than anyone else have recognized. In the order of action, the message had to be completed by something in a different style: that something was *instruction* (*didakhè*).

At a certain moment, which seems most likely to have occurred at the end of a long trip through Galilee, Jesus therefore made the decision to gather round him some disciples (Mk 1 : 16–20, and parallels). Already recognized as a prophet, he now in addition became a *master* (*didaskalos*; Lk: *epistates*, six times). Now for Jesus, becoming master meant first of all giving a new form to his "word"; but it also meant, in the nature of the case, accepting a proportionate modification in his rhythm of activity and even in his style of life.

In the Palestine of his day, indeed, when a master gave instruction to disciples, he did not in any sense make long speeches to them, as lecturers and speakers do today. It would be totally mistaken for us to imagine, for instance, that Jesus' parables were simply "declaimed" like lectures, and that the disciples had only to put together the precious statements afterwards in the light of whatever clear memories might have lodged in their minds as the words flowed along. It is an equally total—and equally serious—mistake to picture the Sermon on the Mount as being like the type of sermon we are familiar with, or to describe it as we read it in Matthew as an "inaugural discourse," or a "program discourse," or an "evangelical discourse." In reality, the Sermon on the Mount is made up of a collection of short "instructions"—each of which, even in its original form, would have been no longer than, say, the Beatitudes (Mt 5 : 3–10 or 12) or the Our Father (Mt 6 : 7–13), and thus having the same modest literary proportions as most of the parables.

We must realize that these things are now very far away. To understand the kind of activity Jesus was performing as "master" calls for a short explanation. "Instruction," in fact, presupposed that the "master" had made a thorough study of the subject, its development, and often even its formulation, for himself. When the time came to pass it on, the instruction thus alread took a definite form. The master would sit and group his disciples around him, and normally they would not be very numerous, for instruction, of its nature, was not intended for the multitude. The "crowd" might be present, as our accounts are often pleased to emphasize, partly no doubt to show what popularity the master had with them. But, even in the presence of the crowd— and one must not exaggerate their numerical size: there could be a "crowd" in ordinary houses (Mk 3 : 32)—it is generally quite clear that it was the attention of his closest disciples (*close* in both senses) that the master chiefly sought. Strictly speaking, then, it was to them that he delivered his instruction.

This he would do by repeating his formulae over and over, until they were firmly fixed in the disciples' minds. Then, once that first memorizing was done, there would be, if circumstances permitted, a period of explanation, with questions and answers.[13] The master could thus be assured that his instruction was not merely remembered, but understood.[14] In short, the instruction was true teaching (*didaskein*) in the manner of time and place, and, if properly received, would lead to a certain "understanding" and a certain "knowledge" (*eidenai, ginoskein*).

In every respect, therefore, the instruction given by Jesus was clearly different from any form of discourse whose only real purpose was persuasion. Consequently, to understand how the parables, or the "instructions" grouped in the Sermon on the Mount, have come down to us in the state they are in, there is no question of having to suppose that Jesus' first hearers were gifted with a miraculous memory, nor that the gospel tradition was produced as a result of some miraculous reconstituting of the past. We need only suppose that Jesus was a "master" admirably equipped for the job—which he was; and that his most faithful hearers were in fact his "disciples"—which they were.

But how different is the *instruction* from the *message*, if we compare them? The message was for any who chanced to hear him; the instruction was above all for the disciples who followed the master wherever he went. The message called for continual and rapid move-

---

[13] Mk 4 : 13–20 and parallels, on the parable of the sower; see also Lk 2 : 46, where Jesus, at the age of twelve, is shown "sitting among the teachers, listening to them and asking them questions."

[14] Mk 4 : 13: "Do you not understand (*ouk oidate*) this parable? How then will you understand (*gnos esthe*) all the parables?"

ment from place to place, on Jesus' part; whereas the instruction, though not keeping him on one spot, like a schoolmaster, nonetheless obliged him to slow down the rhythm of his activity very considerably.

We must not exaggerate the differences, however. The instruction, though subordinate to the message, was at the same time coordinated with it, as we see especially in the parables of the kingdom. The opening made in the hope of the people of Galilee by the stunning blow of the message must in some way be made wide enough by the instruction, slow and patient, in order finally to make room for the entry of the whole of the "good news." Though there is no text that spells it out for us, it would seem that such was Jesus' intention when, at the end of his first Galilean trip, he gathered a group of disciples, to whom his word took the form of instruction. The master's idea here is clear from the facts, and one need only point to them.

It may, on the other hand, be thought that the close relationship between the message and the instruction, despite some inevitable disjointedness, made possible a wide and deep continuity in both forms of activity and style of life. The instruction in itself certainly called for a degree of stability,[15] but Jesus was certainly as remote as it was possible to be from any spirit of system. Even after adopting the "master-disciple" structure, he always preserved great freedom of movement. Perhaps the most significant evidence we have of this is the reply he made one day to the stranger who declared himself ready to "follow" him wherever he went: "Foxes have holes, and the birds of the air have nests, but the Son of man has nowhere to lay his head."[16] Perhaps this was a slight exaggeration, but it made it clear that "following" him was no sinecure. I have tried to trace the outline of Jesus' activity by way of the division between the two chief literary forms, message and instruction. In fact, these literary forms are not abstract entities, growing out of mere chance historical contingency. In Jesus' thinking and speaking, they were truly means of action, deliberately chosen and developed in view of one common end which could be defined as the decisive inauguration of the kingdom of God.

These means of action, in their turn, naturally dictated a certain style of life to anyone who was regularly making use of them. Taken

---

[15] Mk 4 : 13; 9 : 1, speak of his "dwelling" in Capharnaum, "his own city."
[16] Lk 9 : 57–8. Mt 8 : 19–20 shows the incident relating to an already sympathetic scribe.

as a whole, the contents of both message and instruction, the goal aimed at, the means used, and a certain style which all these things imposed on his daily attitudes and movements, combined to provide the figure of Jesus with certain easily identifiable characteristics from the start: he was *prophet* and he was *master*, and he could be both at the same time.[17] Later on, but only later on, a further step was taken, in the recognition that this prophet and master also had a messianic quality.

The dividing line between the literary forms which has governed our analysis, therefore, was not a frontier, still less a barrier. In fact there is something rather disconcerting in the freedom with which the gospel tradition moves from one to the other.[18] However, it is not impossible, given the necessary attentiveness, to find one's way about in it, and ultimately the picture which emerges remains a fairly clear one.

Against the background of this picture, we can see the original and authentic meaning of a number of Jesus' statements which have had a tremendous influence upon our conception of the style of life suitable to the pastoral ministry. I want now to make that meaning clear in the light of the analysis I have made.

Let us look first at the episode of the "rich young man" (Mt 19: 16–22; Mk 10 : 17–22; Lk 18 : 18–23). Mark, in his accounts, says simply, "a man." Luke speaks of "a ruler," which suggests a mature man with some responsibility. Matthew first follows Mark in his account, but ends by saying more precisely that he was "a young man." We need not get involved in problems of translation, for in Greek the "young man" is a *néaniskos*, and a *néaniskos* is not an adolescent (*meirakion*), nor even necessarily a very young man; it could mean a man of twenty, or equally a man of thirty or more, and could in any case mean someone already involved in obligations and responsibilities of different kinds.[19]

---

[17] Mt 11 : 1: "When Jesus had finished instructing his twelve disciples"— this was the first sending of the Twelve—"he went on from there to teach and preach (*didaskein kai kerussein*) in their cities." See also Mk 6 : 6, with *didaskon* only; Lk 8 : 1: "Soon afterward he went on through cities and villages, preaching and bringing the good news of the kingdom of God"—which might be better rendered, perhaps, as "announcing the good news as a herald" (*kerusson kai euaggélizoménos*).

[18] See, for example, Mt 4 : 23–5, after the calling of the first disciples; and Lk 4 : 15.

[19] Acts 7 : 58: at the time of Stephen's martyrdom, only a short time before his conversion, Paul is described by Luke as *néanias*, which means the same. One may point out by the way that there is thus no reason to make Matthew's "young

Well, then, a "young man" presents himself to Jesus, and, greeting him respectfully with his title, "master," asks him what "good deed" he must do "to have eternal life." Jesus answers, "If you would enter life, keep the commandments." I have kept them, the young man replies; "what do I still lack?"

> Jesus said to him, "If you would be perfect, go, sell what you possess, and give to the poor, and you will have treasure in heaven; and come, follow me." When the young man heard this he went away sorrowful, for he had great possessions. [Mt 19 : 16–22.]

It is not part of my purpose to analyze the whole of this story in detail; from the standpoint we are concerned with here there are only two points we must dwell on: "if you would be perfect" (given only in Matthew), and "come, follow me." The two are in fact connected, and what matters is to understand the connection aright.

In exegetic as well as pastoral interpretation, there is a certain tendency to make a direct connection between the call to "perfection" and the renunciation of riches. But was that what Jesus meant? I imagine that everyone would agree that the essence of the master's reply is the *come, follow me.* In the context in which the story is told to us, "to follow" Jesus as "master" was primarily to attach oneself to him to hear his teaching—or, if you prefer the language of the evangelical tradition, his "instruction." But since, on the other hand, the invitation containing the phrase *if you would be perfect* occurs only in Matthew, the best way of finding what it means is to examine Matthew himself.

In effect, it does not take a long search to find in Matthew "instructions" given by Jesus relating to the "perfection" of the commandments, and in a more general way, to the "perfection" of the law. We find them in the Sermon on the Mount, where in fact they are presented expressly as such:

> Think not that I have come to abolish the law and the prophets; I have come not to abolish them but to fulfill them. [5 : 17.]
> You have heard that it was said to the men of old, "You shall not kill; . . ." But I say to you that every one who is angry with his brother shall be liable to judgment. [5 : 21-2.]

---

man" the type of the adolescent who refuses his "vocation" in order to have the advantage of a fine, and possibly lucrative, career. This is a most unjustified slur on the memory of a generous man, and in addition confuses a good many issues that would be better served by lucidity and honesty.

You, therefore, must be perfect, even as your heavenly Father is perfect. [5 : 48.][20]

We see, then, how, in determining to "follow" Jesus, one may look further than the commandments themselves for a greater "perfection" which is, in essence, an imitation of the Father, and it is Jesus' "instruction" which outlines that imitation for those who become his "disciples."

There is, therefore, a direct link between the invitation to "perfection" which Jesus addresses to the "young man", and the invitation to "follow" him which he extends at the same time. The link is to be found in the "master's instruction" which actually proposes a greater "perfection" than that of the commandments which the "young man" declares himself to have observed "from his youth."[21]

But from then on it is equally clear that to abandon one's riches becomes a precondition of freedom to "follow" Jesus and receive his teaching, rather than by any direct link a condition of "perfection" itself. One does not become "perfect" by the mere fact of giving up one's riches and distributing them to the poor (see 1 Cor 13 : 3). One becomes so by becoming pupil to a "master" whose "instruction" teaches mercy and love before all else.[22] But to follow Jesus, and thus become fully his disciple, one must first be free, or become free, to do so. There are times when that freedom may even require that one give up one's goods and distribute them to the poor; and furthermore, whoever goes to that extreme can sustain his hope with the thought that a "treasure" is prepared for him in heaven.

On the other hand, there are also certain established situations which it is proper to respect. The "young man" Jesus met had great possessions; when suddenly faced with an invitation to "follow" him, he must have decided that he was not free to do so, and "went away sorrowful". It is surely no betrayal of the love Jesus himself felt for this stranger (Mk 10 : 21) to impute honorable motives to his decision. What possible right have we to do anything else? Who are we to

---

[20] Note that the order in which the commandments are recalled to the "young man" in 19 : 18–19 is precisely the same, apart from two additions in the one and one in the other, as that laid out in the corresponding "instructions" of the Sermon on the Mount.

[21] Mk 10 : 20; Lk 18 : 21. With the invitation to "perfection" in Mt 19 : 21, compare in Mark and Luke the phrases *one thing* and *one thing you still lack*: the sense is the same, though the allusion to Jesus' distinctive "instruction" is less clear.

[22] See, for example, Lk 6 : 36: "Be merciful, even as your Father is merciful."

do such a thing? The accounts we have say nothing of his reasons, still less do they analyze them: they stop simply at the consideration of the riches, and the obstacles these can place to any higher aspiration. Yet ultimately, "with God all things are possible" (Mt 19 : 26), and even the aspirations of the rich may one day be fulfilled.

There are further subtleties here which demand careful recognition. The story does not include, strictly speaking, any invitation to be detached from wealth: there is—something quite different—an invitation to "follow" Jesus which in itself generally presupposes the widest possible liberty, for it is clear that one cannot be at once in one's own home, among one's own people, arranging one's affairs, and at the same time out on the roads, going from town to town, village to village and house to house, wholly devoted to the "word" that announces and inaugurates the kingdom, and showing in addition, by the very fact of being with Jesus, that the kingdom of God is effectively inaugurated already. To "follow" Jesus, at that time, did not yet mean withdrawing into the desert or, as we sometimes put it, leaving the "world" in order to "practise the evangelical virtues." On the contrary, it meant being willing to be with Jesus in the very middle of towns, in the middle of villages, in the middle of houses, in the middle of the "crowd"—reaping the "word," being the yeast put into the dough (Mt 13 : 33; Lk 13 : 20–21), and thus making a concrete gesture in proof that the "good news" of limitless hope is there, at work, recognizable, among men (Lk 17 : 21).

At bottom, then, what governed the whole complexus of conditions of freedom for the disciples of the first hour was, for Jesus, the "service of the word", of that "word" which was the "good news" of the hope contained in the very words "kingdom of God", of that "word" which must not merely be welcomed, but taken to oneself, and spread to others at every opportunity[23]—a word which vitally needed from the first to be given a permanent and concrete witness of, quite simply, presence. Hence some form of giving up one's goods must be among the conditions of freedom required for the "ministry of the word."

As we see from the example of the Twelve and of Jesus himself, this giving up could, and in fact did, take varying forms, depending on the circumstances. The Twelve had "left all things" (Mt 19 : 27, and

[23] The first short-term mission of the Twelve, which seems to have been followed by one on a much larger scale, of which however only Luke seems to have made a record (10 : 1–20).

elsewhere) to "follow" Jesus. This does not prevent our finding on several occasions Simon and Andrew, James and John, in their boats, laboring as they had in their previous situations. It seems, too, as if at least for a time Jesus himself had a home in Capharnaum where he had decided to settle temporarily (Mt 4 : 13; 9 : 1). At the moment of death, we find him handing over the care of his own mother to the "disciple" he loved best; and "from that hour the disciple took her to his own home" (Jn 19 : 27). The meaning of this is clear.

And what advantage could there be in destroying existing situations to make them fit into a framework of "principles"? It does not seem as if Jesus ever let himself be lured into any such perilous undertaking. The giving up of one's goods was one condition among others for the "service of the word": it was not an object in itself before which all other considerations must in all circumstances give away.

A second declaration of Jesus, which the gospel tradition connects with the meeting of the "rich young man," takes us on from this point to the real heart of the problem. This time, in fact, it is not merely possessions which are in question, but also the closest family relationships: father, mother, brothers, sisters, wife, and children.

The "young man" departs, and Jesus openly expressed his distress. Looking beyond the personal situation of this "young man," he sees riches as a heaping up of obstacles to obstruct "entry" to the kingdom. "It is easier," he says, "for a camel to go through the eye of a needle than for a rich man to enter the kingdom of God." The image was stark, indeed, and the disciples were horrified, but Jesus calmed them by pointing out that what seems impossible to men is not so to God. It was at this point that Peter, evidently curious to know whether the opposite held true, interjected:

"Lo, we have left everything (*aphekamen panta*) and followed you (*ekolouthesamen soi*). What then shall we have?" And Jesus said to them, "Truly, I say to you, in the new world, when the Son of man shall sit on his glorious throne, you who have followed me (*humeis hoi akolouthesantes moi*) will also sit on twelve thrones, judging the twelve tribes of Israel [only in Mt]. And every one who has left (*apheken*) houses [Luke here adds 'or wife'] or brothers or sisters or father or mother or children or lands for my name's sake [Mk: 'for my sake and for the gospel'; Lk: 'for the sake of the kingdom of God'], will receive a hundredfold, and inherit eternal life." [Mt 20 : 23-9; cf. Mk 10 : 23–30; Lk 18 : 24-30.]

Once again I have inserted the Greek words into the translation. For there are places, in fact, when it is not certain that a more or less unconscious transposition does not take place in our minds, even before we can be reasonably sure of having begun to understand the text. Granted, we read here *leave* and there *follow*. But these concrete verbs which had a very clearly defined meaning in the minds of Jesus' first disciples, because for them they expressed a living experience, do not speak anything like so forcefully to our present-day feeling and imagination. Thus, though we read *leaving* and *following*, what we immediately—or pretty soon—take these to mean is *renunciation* and *detachment*, for these are things familiar to us; this is well-known ground, and we imagine we have therefore understood. Yet in neither case are they the same human realities, and we would certainly do well to be rather more hesitant than we are in thus interpreting them.

We should devote special attention to the nuances of the terms used by the gospel narrators, for they are dealing here not simply with houses and fields, but with people, and people who are already bound together at the most basic level in the family circle. It is quite one thing, after all, to "leave" a father, mother, brother, sisters, wife, and children, quite another to be "detached" from them, and obviously something different again to turn such "detachment" into a kind of ideal.

Certainly "leaving," in the perspective of the first disciples, meant ratifying a choice between two orders of values, and in that sense it meant detaching oneself (see Lk 14 : 25–7). But it is equally clear that there was a limit to that "detachment." One did not "leave" because "leaving" was good in itself, but because it was seen as better, in the circumstances, to "follow" Jesus. One "left" because the "good news" of the kingdom (Mk) demanded it at that moment. Ultimately, then, this step was determined by the "service of the word", and found its proper balance in relation to that "service."

Could it have been because they were especially attentive to that balance that Mark and Matthew failed to include *wife* in their list? Possibly, though silence is always hard to interpret.[24] On the other hand, it is quite impossible to see Luke's inclusion of *wife* as indicating celibacy as an ideal. Such an interpretation—which has recently been attempted—can only be made by overlooking the most well-

---

[24] There are a few manuscripts of Mark and Matthew in which this is not the case, but they seem unlikely to represent the original text.

established rules of grammar, and also by ignoring the whole of the context.

In any case, and far more significantly, it must be noted that Jesus' statement is related, not to sexuality as such, but to the totality of family relationships. In short, what is demanded by the service of the "good news" of the kingdom, is a general state of freedom, one of the conditions for which will ultimately involve an abandonment of married life. There is absolutely no suggestion here that the exercise of sexuality, as such, might be in any way unfitting to the "service of the word." The question is considered from the standpoint of the whole style of life, and it is that that matters.

This brings us back again to our earlier conclusions. One could not, at that time, "follow" Jesus without at the same time adopting his style of life, which involved being ready to "leave" many people and many things.[25] But, here again, the concrete forms this could take were endlessly more flexible than a perfunctory reading of the accounts might lead us to suppose. We have to allow a lot for stylization: the gospels are not biographies in which we can hope to find the detailed analysis so dear to our historians.

Lastly, there is a third statement of Christ's with a direct bearing on our study. We find it only in Matthew, which suggests at least that it did not receive as much attention from tradition as those we have just been looking at. Then, too, the literary situation in which Matthew places it in his account does not seem to be so clear as to be closed to different interpretations, and to this extent the situation in which it was said escapes us, with the result that the context throws little light on the interpretation.

Let us, however take things as we find them. To present Jesus with a quandary, some Pharisees asked him a question about divorce. His answer appeared so exacting that the disciples were led to declare: "If such is the case of a man with his wife, it is not expedient to marry" (Mt 19 : 10). Then, according to Matthew, Jesus carried the question on to different ground by replying:

Not all men can receive this precept, but only those to whom it is given. For there are eunuchs who have been so from birth, and there are eunuchs who have been made eunuchs by men, and there are eunuchs who have made themselves eunuchs for the sake of the king-

[25] See the calling of the first "disciples," Mk 1 : 16–20, etc.

dom of heaven (*dia ten basileian ton ouranon*). He who is able to receive this, let him receive it. [Mt 19 : 11–12.]

The image itself is clear enough: it refers to continence, and to continence freely chosen. It refers also to an exceptional situation: only those "to whom it is given" can understand the cost of the choice. Evidently they are rare, though no more explicit value-judgement is made upon the fact.

Since the verb is in the past—"there are eunuchs who *have been made eunuchs*"—we can further presume that Jesus was alluding to cases already known, and here interpreters have often suggested John the Baptist, which is likely enough. But must we go on from this to follow the image to the ultimate conclusion of believing that Jesus was thinking not merely of voluntary continence, but of permanent continence? In itself this would seem natural, and it is indeed extremely possible. But we must recognize the fact that we have little evidence to go on. If one prefers to keep to a more general meaning, all that can be said is that Jesus is proposing here, in a new form, something we have already heard as to the conditions of freedom necessary to "follow" him and thus place oneself at the service of the kingdom and of the word (Mt 19 : 27–9, and parallels).

But is this to blunt the edge of Jesus' statement, which under the form of this image seems precisely to want to carry the thing further, though with great reservation? All in all, it seems more likely that Jesus *was* thinking here of permanent continence, freely chosen. But, it is also quite clear that this continence, whatever form we take it to have, is ultimately linked with a wider action whose scope we have already considered: that of "leaving houses, brothers, sisters, father, mother (wife), children, or fields" for Jesus' sake (Mk: "my sake"; Mt: "my name's sake"), for the "kingdom of God" (Lk), and for the sake of the "good news" (Mt 19 : 29, and parallels). And it is this that is the core of the whole thing.

Everyone has his own special gift, and no gift should be rejected, none despised. The permanent does not outshine the temporary, nor does the total render the partial useless. For all is ordered to serving the hope of the "kingdom" (Mt 19 : 12), whose ways are numberless indeed, if it be true that, in this order, a mere cup of water (Mt 10 : 42; Mk 9 : 41) wins a place of honor along with the greatest labors.

3

Home and Marriage in the Itinerant Service of the Word

I have purposely avoided speaking of Jesus exercising a *ministry*, nor will I speak of an apostolic *ministry*. I must make it clear that in rejecting a term everyone uses I am not just following some philological mannerism of my own, or a passing technical scruple. In our theological and pastoral vocabulary, *ministry* has taken on a markedly institutional sense, in which the dominant note seems that of organized religion. One has only to mention the "priestly ministry," the "ministry of preaching," or the "ministry of the sacraments" to evoke in the mind movements, attitudes, behavior and styles and states of life, whose outlines, both to laymen and clerics, are immediately determined by an omnipresent ecclesial institution. We are at once in the world of vocations and missions of definite rules of preparation and execution, of assignments and directives, conditions of licitness and validity—not forgetting a whole important system of sanctions: in short, a large and extremely rich heritage of various structures, some large, some small, some universal, some local, some permanent, some transitory, within which every individual's life must take its place.

Of course, the institutional framework of the ministry, though attentive to a certain regularity in even our least actions, still leaves room for many initiatives and original creations in which each one's gifts, and the gifts of the community find great scope. We may even say that, ideally at least, the institutional framework of the ministry actually requires such creations and initiatives, and that without them it would soon lose all contact with the movement of real life. On the other hand, it would simply contradict the facts to claim that it is first and foremost this which the vocabulary of *ministry* brings to mind.

It goes without saying, too, that this was not so at the beginning. And yet we do not hesitate to speak of the prophetic ministry, of the ministry of John, the ministry of Jesus, the ministry of the gospel, the apostolic ministry, and many others; indeed, we find it convenient to do so, since this corresponds to an idea with which we are very familiar. Now it seems to me that we do not always succeed in avoiding anachronisms here. We unwittingly project on to the past things which belong to our world rather than to it. And there seems to me to be the most glaring anachronism in the way we speak of the ministry and preaching of Jesus and of his immediate disciples. The result is that what we look for in our origins is often simply what we want to find in them, which may not in fact be there at all, or if it is there, may easily not be there in the form in which we imagine it. By this blunder, we are missing a considerable part of the riches of early tradition whose creative possibilities, I need hardly say, are far from being exhausted.

In fact, if we read them carefully, we soon find that the apostolic writings make little use of the *ministry* vocabulary to describe the actions of Jesus and his immediate disciples. What we do discover very soon, on the other hand, is the tremendous flexibility, and also the great variety, of terms taken from the most "uninstitutionalized" language of the day, the language of "activity" and of "service." I shall therefore continue here to use these terms in order as far as possible to ensure a true perception of the values they represented at the time.

It is vital to make clear from the start one fact whose significance will become more evident as we go on. It is this: that the "service of the word," in the apostolic era, was extraordinarily diversified, as regards the people who took part in it, the literary forms they made use of, and the general conditions in which it took place.

Of the people, obviously we will think first of the apostles, and especially of the Twelve, though we know almost nothing of either the style or the sphere of activity of most of them. Yet, in fact, the Twelve were not the only ones to bear the title and fill the function of apostles —a first indication of the flexibility with which changes and developments took place. Paul and Barnabas are the best-known examples, but there were others, as we see particularly in the *Didache* (11 : 3–

6). The service taken on by Apollos sometime in the fifties of the first century is not well defined, but he must also certainly have been very close to the apostolic way of life.[1]

The first "deacons" (*diakonoi*) in Jerusalem were established for a service (*diakonia*) of beneficence, in order that the Twelve might not be diverted from their own unique service by other tasks which were in danger of absorbing them (Acts 6 : 1–6). But we soon find Stephen and Philip, each in his own way, taking part in the "service of the word." Stephen frequently entered into "disputes" with various groups of Hellenized Jews in Jerusalem (Acts 6 : 9–10). Philip, after the persecution which killed his companion, went away and took to the road, as many others were also obliged to do. The dispersal was most fruitful, for some of those dispersed took advantage of the occasion by setting about spreading the "word of the good news" wherever they went. It was thus, in particular, that a town in Samaria received Philip, and he seems to have stayed there for some time. The former "deacon" of Jerusalem "preached (*ekerussen*) to them the Christ," and signs came to confirm his message.[2]

Then, following these dispersed Christians turned by circumstances into heralds of the "good news," we find prophets and doctors coming forward who, in varying forms, set themselves in their turn to the "service of the word."[3] Some among these were itinerants; some stayed in one place. There were men, of course, but we are sometimes inclined to forget that there were women, too.

Meanwhile, the "deacon" Philip had settled in Caesarea, where he worked from then on as an "evangelist" (see also 2 Tim 4 : 5; Eph 4 : 11), and Luke notes in passing that his four daughters, unmarried and living with him, were prophetesses (Acts 21 : 8–9). We learn from the same source that Apollos, in Ephesus, received further instruction from the couple, Priscilla and Aquila, then living in the town (Acts 18 : 24–6). As far as we know, neither of these had any definite title in the "service of the word," which makes it all the more interesting, from our point of view, to find them "expounding," on occasion, things relating to faith or the Christian life to such a man as Apollos.

Though we cannot possibly list them all, surely we must also men-

---

[1] 1 Cor 1 : 12; 3 : 5, "What then is Apollos? What is Paul? Servants (*diakonoi*) through whom you believed as the Lord assigned to each"; see also 3 : 22.

[2] Acts 8 : 1, 4–8; also 11 : 19–21, showing the birth of the church in Antioch in similar conditions resulting from the same dispersal.

[3] Acts 11 : 27, for Jerusalem; 13 : 1–3, for Antioch.

tion here those who were the apostles' travelling-companions and col-
laborators: Mark, Luke, Timothy, Titus, Sylvanus, Epaphras, and so
many others. Nor should we forget those less well-known workers in
the "service of the word" who used their hands, their knowledge of
languages, and even (it seems) sometimes the advantages of their
written style, in the service of setting out the apostolic letters—that
Tertius, for instance, who was Paul's secretary while he was preparing
his great letter to the Christians of Rome (Rom 16 : 22). It is also
noteworthy that that same letter, the most important Paul wrote, was
undoubtedly carried to its readers by a woman, the same Phoebe,
deaconess of Cenchreae, who had already shown herself a most generous and effective "helper of many and of myself as well" (Rom 16 :
1–2).

We find a similar diversity and flexibility in the various forms of the
"word." First, and most significant, we find no servile imitation of the
literary forms previously adopted by Jesus, and therefore no auto-
matic reproduction of the style of activity which those same literary
forms might have represented. Obviously there is a recognizable relationship between the original "message" of Jesus and the first apostolic "message," at least as the latter is presented to us by Luke in
Acts,[4] and glimpsed in the epistles of Paul and elsewhere. But even
so, the differences are considerable, involving equally considerable
changes in the apostolic style of activity.

The devlopment that was taking place was, in fact, in the direction
of discursive presentation: something not present at all either in Jesus'
own initial "message" (Mk 1 : 14–15), or in the "message" the
Twelve took on their first mission, which was substantially the same,
both in form and content, as that of Jesus' himself (Mk 6 : 12; Mt 10 :
7; Lk 9 : 2, 6; see also 10 : 9). The original *kerugma* was now
tending to become what we may call "kerygmatic discourse."[5]

Similar changes occurred in relation to "instruction." No one in the
apostolic generation seems to have continued using Jesus' "parable"
as a literary form. They were content to preserve it as a memory, and
in this way the "parable" remained the distinctive mark of Jesus' own
"instruction." On the other hand, the apostles' "instruction" seems in
general to have evolved into a distinctly more exhortatory or recom-
mendatory style than their master's ever had. There are many ex-

---

[4] Notably 2 : 14–36 and 13 : 16–41.
[5] Acts 10 : 34–43—though here, it is true, the scene is an ordinary home
(that of the non-Jewish centurion, Cornelius).

amples of this kind of "instruction" in the New Testament epistles.[6] Then, too, there was prophetic "instruction" to add its special quality of reprimand and encouragement, as in the letters to the churches of Asia Minor (Rev 2 : 1–3; 22), of visions of suffering and consolation, as in the rest of the Revelation to John.[7] We know much less of the "instruction" of the doctors, but we can form some idea of it from the Epistle of James.

Furthermore, despite the importance we must attach to the "message" and the "instruction" of the apostles, it would be a serious mistake on our part to think of them as being the whole field of action in the early service of the word. We are all too ready to talk of the "preaching" of the apostles, and indeed of that of Jesus himself. It is a vague term which always brings a certain anachronism into our thinking, and has in addition the grave disadvantage of effectively masking a whole area of reality as regards the early service of the word. By using it, we distort and impoverish what should be the best models for our own pastoral service.

In fact, the circumstances in which such "kerygmatic discourses" as that of Peter in Jerusalem (Acts 2 : 14–36) and that of Paul in Antioch of Pisidia (Acts 13 : 16–43) could appear natural must have been extremely rare. We must rather presume, in the normal course of apostolic activity, that both the "message" and the "instruction" took literary forms far closer to conversation and discussion than any kind of lecturing. But of course the "kerygmatic discourses" could be reconstituted in outline and recorded by the narrator of Acts, whereas conversations and discussions dealing with the "message" could not.

A similar comment must be made in regard to "instruction." The instances we have of it in the New Testament epistles represent only the loftier examples of this literary form—precisely those suited to the assemblies and churches to which the epistles were addressed. We have no record of individual "instructions" or "instructions" to small family groups. Yet we know for certain that these shorter forms of both "message" and "instruction," because of their great flexibility and commonness, played a major role in the early service of the word, especially within the home.

I have already referred to the example of the "disputes" the

---

[6] Rom 12 : 1–15; 13, etc.; however 1 Cor 7 : 1–14; 40 is more "disciplinary in tone."

[7] Note that the author, John (Rev 1 : 4, 9) presents himself as a "prophet," not as an apostle (Rev 22 : 9, 18).

"deacon" Stephen had with various groups of Hellenized Jews in his area. Characteristically, Luke puts a long "discourse" into Stephen's mouth at the moment of appearing before his judges, but he makes it fairly clear that it was the "discussions" which in fact led to his arrest (Acts 6 : 8–53). Or, to take another example, when the eunuch of the queen of Ethiopia was baptized by the "deacon" Philip on the way from Jerusalem to Gaza, it was during the course of an ordinary conversation that Philip "told him the good news of Jesus" (Acts 8 : 26–39). Here we find the "message" in its most familiar form—that of dialogue.

It is easy enough to go on from this to imagine a great many intermediate forms in which this could often have taken place in a domestic context (see by implication Eph 6 : 15). But we do not need to think up many hypotheses; for we know, from the best possible source, that Paul normally transmitted his "message" and gave his "instruction," not only in public (*demosiai*), which would have been primarily in the assemblies where the *ekklesia* was to be found, but also in private (*kat' oikous*), that is "in the home of each"—or "from house to house"— as the occasion presented itself (Acts 20 : 20–21). The forms of the "service of the word" and the style of apostolic activity were thus in fact of such a kind that at any moment when it seemed suitable, the "message" and the "instruction" could be brought directly to the individual in the most usual and natural framework of his life—his own home.

Correspondingly, as we have seen, it would be to misunderstand totally the concrete conditions in which the "service of the word" took place in those early days if we were to imagine apostles, prophets, and doctors as being continually in the oratorical attitudes required by more or less imposing assemblies and more or less ceremonial circumstances. Flexibility was, one might say, the rule, in choosing the conditions for carrying out the service of the word.

From time to time the great gatherings in the Temple in Jerusalem were made use of (Acts 3 : 11–26). Far more often the apostles took advantage of the synagogue assemblies on the sabbath, just as Jesus himself had done.[8] And obviously the Christian assemblies were also most important (Acts 2 : 42; 20 : 7–12, etc.). In Athens we find Paul "arguing" (*dielegeto*), not only with the Jews and sympathizers he could fine in the synagogue, but also "every day" with passers-by in

---

[8] Acts 13 : 14–45; 14 : 1; 17 : 2, 17, etc; compare 16 : 12–15.

that great center of attraction, the *agora*, which, as we know, resulted in his giving his famous—and unique—discourse before the Areopagus (Acts 17 : 16–33; compare 14 : 13–18).

But we must not forget that the Temple and the Areopagus were, each in its own way, exceptional places. Nor was the synagogue always welcoming, as we know. And the Christian *ekklesia* could not always be ready to meet together at any moment. Thus it was in fact in the setting of private homes that the service of the word, in all its forms, originally found its most accessible, most frequent, and certainly also its most favourable base. In particular, as was natural, the endless advantages that a home had to offer, as regards hospitality, social relationships, and human contacts, seem to have been spontaneously recognized from the first, both by those who offered and by those who received hospitality.

The incident of the baptism of the centurion Cornelius is, in this respect, extremely significant. In the few days before Peter's arrival, Cornelius had "invited," or "called together" (*sugkalesamenos*) for the occasion 'his kinsmen and close friends' (*tous suggeneis autou kai tous anagkaious philous*). When Peter appeared, therefore, with his companions and the escort Cornelius had sent for him, it was not only the centurion himself who was ready to hear him, but "all his household" (*pas ho oikos*) (Acts 11 : 14)—in other words, not merely his immediate family and his servants, but also the "kinsmen" and "friends" who had been asked for the occasion (Acts 10 : 1–48). After everyone had received baptism, Peter was invited to spend several more days among them. This was in the best traditions of hospitality of the time, and in this way occasions multiplied for giving both "instruction" and "the message."

This seems to me to provide a wonderfully detailed and concrete example of the way in which the first kernel of many a Christian *ekklesia* must have been formed in the early days. It also shows us the precise locus, the precise place, in which the "service of the word" was articulated in the *ekklesia* of the apostolic age. Though we hardly advert to the fact nowadays, there is no doubt that in this respect the "home" played a vitally important role.[9]

[9] In this context see also the shorter account of the baptism of Lydia, the "seller of purple goods" from Thyatira: "The Lord opened her heart to give heed to what was said by Paul. And when she was baptized, with her household (*kai ho oikos autes*), she besought us saying, 'If you have judged me to be faithful to the Lord, come to my house and stay.' And she prevailed upon us" (Acts 16 :

Closely linked as the itinerant service of the word was with domestic life, upon which it depended so largely for its effectiveness and continuity, there is nothing to indicate that in apostolic times it was at the same time generally urging any different ideal—of continence, or of virginity—upon those who became Christ's disciples. What possible reason would it have had for doing so?

In effect, it was only from the comfortable distance of several generations that the writers of the second- and third-century apostolic "novels" (the *Acts* of John, of Paul, of Peter, of Andrew, and of Thomas) could imagine any such thing. But then, this pious bric-à-brac of unnecessary prodigies and sexual obsessions seems to have made a point of challenging the most elementary probabilities. One can hardly expect it to provide any insight into the reality of history—nor indeed into reality of any kind—apart from the evidence it unintentionally gives of the tremendous dualist agony of the time. The genuine documents as a whole, on the other hand, would rather lead us to think that the first disciples of Jesus went no further on the matter than the extremely careful limits held to by their master himself.

However, the "servants of the word," and above all the apostles, were in this respect in a somewhat special situation. It would seem as though Jesus spoke of two forms of continence in the more general context of serving the "good news." On the one hand, there was the continence of those married men who "left" all things to "follow" him, and, on the other, the continence of those who had given up the whole idea of marriage "for the sake of the kingdom" of God. Ultimately, in both cases, continence appeared as simply a condition for service.

What in fact happened as far as the apostles, those chiefly responsible for the itinerant service of the word, were concerned? Can it be discovered? We must realize for a start that to ask the question would certainly seem slightly indiscreet in the eyes of the apostolic generation. For it is itself extremely significant that primitive tradition did not choose to inform the general public about what the apostles may have left behind them. All in all, from where we stand, we must pay homage to that perfect reserve, which remains a clear sign for us of a true estimation of the values involved.

On the other hand, we cannot ignore the fact that the example of

---

12–15). See, too, Acts 16 : 29–34 (the "house" of the jailer of Paul and Silas at Philippi in Macedonia); Acts 18 : 8 (the "household" of Crispus, rulers of the synagogue in Corinth); and 1 Cor 1 : 16 (the "household" of Stephanas, in the same city).

the apostles still, and rightly, inspires the whole style of our own pastoral service; it is important, therefore, to discover what that example was. And it is no bad thing to get as clear a picture of it as we can, if only for the minor advantage of pruning the numbers of approximations we keep making. It seems certain that the truth about the past still has much light to throw on our present-day pastoral service. Within certain limits, imposed by our inability to turn the clock back, a return to the past is healthy and desirable. I cannot, on the other hand, see what real advantage we can get from any of the extras, especially when these are pure and simple legends.

The question is not new; indeed it may even have come to seem almost futile. But we must ask it in our turn, for there are myths still attaching to it: Were the apostles married? From the almost total silence of early tradition on the point, Tertullian dared to draw the quite unwarranted conclusion that, with the exception of Peter, whose mother-in-law was, as we know, cured by Jesus, the apostles either remained celibate, or lived in continence. He, of course, had montanism on the brain.[10] Basil, a man of moderation, though never accused of oversimplifying, was quite content to accept that all the apostles had once been married. He even put them forward as an example to the Christians of his time for whom the arduous paths of asceticism were not attractive.[11]

The truth probably lies somewhere between the two extremes. For if the chance of her having a fever had not happened to bring Jesus to see Peter's mother-in-law, the gospel tradition would in fact have observed total silence on the disciples' marriage. Could we therefore conclude that not one of them was married? No, we could not. All we can say is this: the ideas and the customs of the time and place are enough to make it probable that most of the apostles were married; it is even quite possible that they all were, without exception.

In the absence of any definite evidence, there is no point in speculating on the "virginity" of John in particular, as some among us are wont to do, making his supposed virginity the reason not only for Jesus' preferring him over the other disciples, but even for the depth of vision we find in the fourth gospel! It must honestly be admitted that all this is sheer imagination, which has lost much of its poetry, and is indeed more than a little odd. In actual fact it was not John, but Peter, who seems to have been the first and keenest in feeling

[10] Tertullian, *Demonogamia*, 8.
[11] Basil, *De renuntiatione saeculi*, 1.

Jesus' messianic character at the beginning (Mk 8 : 27–30, and parallels). We must certainly also add here that it is equally untenable to make the so-called "virgin" apostle the Christian symbol for the "function" of contemplation. The truth is that we know nothing at all as to the celibate or married state of John, son of Zebedee; we are inescapably bound by the limits of mere possibility in either case. Wisdom would dictate that we build nothing too ambitious upon such a foundation.

On the other hand, from two phrases from his own authorship, we do know something of Paul's situation. The first relates to those Christians already married, to whom he has just made some recommendations in regard to their conjugal life: "I say this by way of concession, not of command" (1 Cor 7 : 6)—in other words, "you must understand that I have spoken as I have in view of your situation, but I would not have tried to force that situation upon you beforehand." For "I wish that all were as I myself am. But [in fact] each has his own special gift from God, one of one kind and one of another" (1 Cor 7 : 7). Paul then goes on to consider the situation of the unmarried and of widows:

> To the unmarried (*tois agamois*) and the widows I say that it is well for them to remain single as I do. But if they cannot exercise self-control, they should marry. For it is better to marry than to be aflame with passion. [1 Cor 7 : 8–9.]

Most interpreters, ancient and modern, take this passage in its entirety to mean that Paul had never married. Yet there are some who do not agree with this. The problem, in effect, is that *agamos* does not simply mean *celibate*: strictly speaking, the *agamos* is the *unmarried*, which also includes, as the word was used, the widower, and the separated or divorced spouse.[12] Thus, what seems at first sight totally clear becomes somewhat less so upon closer inspection.

There is no point in protesting on a priori grounds against the hypothesis that Paul had been married before, as some people naturally rush to do. Facts are facts. What we must recognize is that there is no need for us to diverge from our path to get involved in any such hypothesis. The one thing we know for sure is that, when he wrote the letter to the Corinthians, he was then free from any conjugal ties (the

---

[12] Cor 7 : 11, where *agamos* is used precisely to cover the situation of the "separated" spouse; compare also verse 34.

general sense of *agamos*). On the other hand, his "instruction," as we read it in 1 Cor 7, does make better sense on the hypothesis that he had never been married. Furthermore, everything else that we know about him seems to lead to the same conclusion. This is all that history can tell us, and it seems a suitable stopping place for our present argument too.

From a standpoint not unrelated to that of marriage, it is also useful to define such chronological details as we can of the apostles' "departures." Though almost all the meager information we have about this is indirect, it seems unlikely that the delays which attached to the first apostolic "departures" were always unconnected with the domestic situations of the men concerned. Thus those delays have significance not merely in the history of the beginnings of the church, but also in helping us to form our idea of those first models for our own pastoral service.

Did the Twelve, and even Paul himself, "leave all things"—houses, possessions, father, mother, brothers, sisters, wives and children—just like that, from one minute to the next, without a moment's thought? It seems, on the face of it, highly unlikely. Does the evidence compel us to think that they did?

Above all, we must avoid oversimplifying things in our imagination. When we read: "Go into all the world and preach the gospel . . ." (Mk 16 : 15; compare Mt 28 : 19), are we meant to understand from this that the apostles at once set about dividing the world among them, and at once got ready to leave? As we know, this is a picture that has long been popular, and though of late it has received certain corrections, it seems likely that it still colors the way a lot of people think. Yet the more detailed accounts given by Luke in the Acts give us a more complicated view which, though not intended to contradict the solemn mission which Mark and Matthew show Jesus giving, nevertheless oblige us to see it in the context of the total experience of the early church.

Thus, after Jesus had left them, we find the Twelve first of all settled in Jerusalem. The establishing of the Seven for a service of good works subsidiary to the service of the word, just before AD 35, would seem in itself to imply a relative staying put on the part of the apostles (Acts 6 : 1–6). The "violent persecution" which burst upon the mother church after the martyrdom of Stephen (about AD 36) resulted in the dispersal of a large number of believers over the countryside of Judaea and Samaria. But Luke expressly notes, on this occasion, that the apostles themselves stayed where they were (Acts 8 : 1).

After that date, the scene becomes confused. There is, however, good reason to think that it was somewhere in the forties that the departure of most of the apostles eventually took place. There were exceptions, however. James, brother of John and son of Zebede, was still in Jerusaleem under Agrippa I, who had him killed by the sword in AD 43 or 44 (Acts 12 : 1–2). Peter himself only left the town for any length of time about then (Acts 12 : 18). We find him there again, however, with John, sometime in the fifties, for the conference to decide the conditions under which gentiles were to be received into the church (Acts 15 : 7; Gal 2 : 9).

It may disturb some of our favorite preconceptions to realize it, but even the "departure" of Paul follows a similar pattern. The incident on the road to Damascus probably took place in AD 36 or 37 (Acts 9 : 1–19). For some time afterwards, Paul proclaimed the "good news" in Damascus (Acts 9 : 19–20), and went to "Arabia" only to return to Damascus (Acts 9 : 23–5; Gal 1 : 17). He then went to Jerusalem to visit Peter, and stayed with him there fifteen days (Gal 1 : 18). By then "three years" had passed since his conversion. If we take that "three years" to mean part of a year, a full year, and part of another year—as was often meant by the phrase at that time—this brings us probably to the year 39 for Paul's visit to Peter in Jerusalem.

Since his presence had immediately caused anxiety among a number of people, Paul then went to his native city of Tarsus, in Cilicia (compare, however, Gal 1 : 21), where he stayed for four years, and where Barnabas, who had known him in Jerusalem, came to find him to share his work in the church in Antioch (Acts 11 : 25–6). This was probably in AD 43. It was by then six or seven years after Paul's baptism by Ananias (Acts 9 : 10–19). A year later, Paul at last left with Barnabas for his first great apostolic journey.

As we see, then, neither the "departure" of the Twelve, nor that of Paul, was anything very sudden. There were delays, even very long ones, inspired no doubt by all kinds of considerations of necessity and utility, but also, almost certainly from time to time, by motives of simple convenience. Once again we find the same kind of flexibility in operation that we have noted elsewhere. And, among the considerations of necessity and reasons of convenience, one must certainly allow for a proper attentiveness to existing domestic situations. Everything, in fact, leads us to believe that there was such attentiveness; it is not mentioned in the accounts we have for the simple reason that at that time and in that place it was taken utterly for granted.

However, we would have one piece of more direct information if we could rescue one passing allusion in one of Paul's letters from all ambiguity. Writing to his church in Corinth, in the spring of AD 57, Paul replies to his detractors by recalling the line of conduct he has always made a point of following in carrying out his mission (1 Cor 9 : 1–23). As a herald of the "good news," he says in substance, he also had the right to get his "living from the gospel," as the Lord commanded. However, he feels himself too much bound to that service, not by his own doing but by that of him who has entrusted it to him, to be ready to place any kind of obstacle to it. That is why he has wanted to give his service freely. "Though I am free from all men, I have made myself a slave to all that I might win the more." But in truth, has he not a right to receive the hospitality of the churches for his food and drink?

> Do we not have the right to be accompanied by a sister as wife (*adelphen gunaika*), as the other apostles and the brothers of the Lord and Cephas? Or it is only Barnabas and I who have no right to refrain from working for a living?

If he has refused to take advantage of that right, it has been to avoid any hint of personal interest standing in the way of his relationship with the Corinthians, and any lessening of the effectiveness of our service.

We thus find in passing that, in those years, "the other apostles" —not necessarily only the Twelve!—"and the brothers of the Lord and Cephas" generally took with them an *adelphen gunaika*, and that the churches were responsible for giving them all the usual hospitality. Paul, note, did not follow this custom of the "other apostles"; but he expresses this only in terms of a personal preference resulting from a vivid awareness of the requirements of his service. Thus in rejecting for himself what is a recognized right, he wants to make it clear that he is not imposing any additional obligations on those to whom he is bringing the "good news."

Who would the *adelphe gune* have been? A "Christian," certainly.[13] But whether *gune* meant *wife* or *helper* is not clear; opinions remain divided, and it would be profitless to enter into a long discussion on the point. Both the Greek and Paul's style would allow either sense, depending on the context.

In itself, though, it would appear to be the normal thing for a married apostle to have wanted to take his "wife" with him. Nor is it easy to see why, in effect, an apostle who could always count on being given hospitality (Acts 10 : 48; 16 : 15; etc.) should have needed a "helper" for his daily needs, especially since that "helper" would herself have had first to be received and looked after by someone. The least we can say in the circumstances is that the apostles' task could have received only the slenderest simplification from this form of feminine company. It would surely have been far better to take the simpler way out and accept the ready-made situation of marriage where it existed.[14]

Finally, therefore, it seems to be much more likely that the "sister" here was in fact the Christian wife, and that most of the apostles, from the thirties on, found it most practical if they were married to take their wives with them when they came to set out for their first mission field.[15]

Furthermore, this interpretation, and this custom, both seem to me to be fully in keeping with Jesus' intentions for the service of the word. When he talked of "leaving," he did not mean "abandoning," still less abandoning for good. The point of view whereby Paul justifies his own personal preference is a quite different one. He speaks only of his own freedom of action, upon which point other people

---

[13] *Adelphe* was a "sister" through community of faith; see Rom 16 : 1; 1 Cor 7 : 15; etc.

[14] Lk 8 : 1–3 is dealing with a group, Jesus and the Twelve, and, in addition, a definite material contribution, which places us at once in a quite different situation.

[15] Since facts, rather than theories, are what we must go by, one must in passing mention here the couple Andronicus and Junias, who were apostles "of note," Christians before Paul himself (Rom 16 : 7), and who having no doubt left Jerusalem, probably around AD 35 like so many others (Acts 8 : 1; 11 : 19–21), ended up in Rome around AD 57–8 (on Rom 16 : 7, see Chrysostom, *In Epist. ad Rom*, 31, 2; [PG 60, 670]. To avoid what they saw as a problem—a man and his wife being together recognized as "apostles"!—it is true that some people have put forward the the idea that *Jounias* was an abbreviation of *Iunianus*. Yet this is most unlikely, since there is no evidence that *Iunianus* was a masculine name at all. Without proof to the contrary, it remains preferable to take the text in its normal sense, and to regard Junias as the wife of Andronicus.

might think differently—which he takes for granted in the first place.

At first glance, then, one might be tempted here to carry over our thinking into a different area by bringing into it Paul's instruction on marriage and virginity (1 Cor 7 : 1–40). But that instruction is not in fact directly concerned either with the "service of the word," or with the "service of the assembly."

It comes primarily by way of answer to questions which have been asked earlier by those to whom he is writing. They, in asking them, were not concerned with what seemed to them the most desirable conditions for carrying out the service of the word and of the assembly; nor does Paul's answer suppose anything of the kind. When his line of thought leads him to make a passing reference to his own situation (7 : 7–8), he does so not from the point of view of his service, as in 9 : 5, but from the point of view of his general condition as a man and a Christian.[16]

It is therefore wholly unwarranted to suggest, as has been done, that Paul was here thinking mainly of the condition he would like to see obtaining for episcopi and deacons, the servants of the assembly. When he came to the point of giving an instruction directly to them, he expressed himself quite differently (1 Tim 3 : 1–13; Tit 1 : 5–9); and it is there that we must look for his true ideas on the subject.

[16] Especially 7 : 1: "It is well for a man (*anthropoi*) not to touch a woman"; see, too 29–35.

4

Home and Marriage in the Service of the Assembly

There have been studies beyond number produced on the birth and early development of the church's hierarchy; on the origin, structure, and scope of the first apostolate; on the transmitting of apostolic responsibilities to the presidents of the local churches and their councils of presbyters, the original situation of the episcopate in the presbyteral college, and the part played by deacons in the direct service of the liturgical assembly; and, more recently, on the collegial nature, first of apostolic responsibility, and later on of episcopal responsibility—to mention only the most important points of interest. All these studies, whatever their date of writing, have in themselves the possibility of taking on a very fruitful pastoral significance in relation to our own present situation—as regards both the concrete means of effectively spreading the gospel, and the gathering of Christians into a genuinely evangelical communion. Both are urgent tasks, especially for history and theology, and I certainly have no wish to underestimate in the smallest degree the tremendous scope for renewal that there is in vast sectors of the church's life.

In spite of this, it remains true that awareness of the "hierarchy," keen to start with because of the distinctive heritage of the Roman tradition, and further heightened by the present combination of circumstances, has absorbed too much of our attention, to the detriment of what I might call the "micromorphology" of pastoral service in the early church. At a higher level, we are greatly concerned with the division of functions, powers, and authority. But we are not so ready to look closely at the various concrete conditions which largely went to make up the effectiveness and continuity of pastoral service in the church of old.

How much real attention, for instance, have we given to the domestic context of the original *ekklesia?* Having been virtually blinded to some values by the honour we have attached (whether merited or not) to the institutions adopted by the church over the centuries, we have surely seen in an all too negative way the married state of all those leaders of the "assembly" whose authority we are ever ready to quote upon other points. Let us be honest; being so may also prove an excellent means of being lucid as well.

One final question. How has it come about, among other things, that elements as decisive as the welcome afforded by the *ekklesia,* and even pastoral hospitality, escape our eye when we look at what constituted the extraordinary spring of our origins? Could it really be that we no longer know how to see? Or is it rather that certain sensitivities, which are at times beyond our control, direct our gaze only to where we feel somehow sure in advance of finding only what will confirm us in the choices we have already made? This possibility is my excuse here for trying to fill in some at least of the gaps.

There is one fact of immense pastoral value which strikes us from the first: there was no rigidity, but a most fruitful flexibility attuned to reality, coloring the whole "micromorphology" of the service of the gospel in the early days—both in the itinerant service of the word on the one hand, and in the pastoral service of the assembly on the other, as well as in the close and constant interpenetration between the two in the changing forms dictated by concrete situations.

It would in fact be a distortion of history to stress only the itinerant character of the earliest service of the word. To look only at the most central and best-known area, it is useful to remind ourselves, to start with, that the first departures of the apostles were largely in response to the indications of circumstance. As we know, it is the sheerest contradiction of the facts to picture the apostles as obeying from the first moment totally and in every respect the principle that the "good news" was to be proclaimed to all nations. The reality was more variable, more concerned with immediate needs and immediate possibilities. Neither Jesus nor his first disciples give the impression of having been theorists of action. It is as harmful to pastoral theology as to history, to try to fit their words and actions into some rigid system.

Nor does it seem as though the first bearers of the "good news" were guided by very many rigid principles once they were on their travels. They certainly knew where they were going—in every sense. But it is easy to see at the same time that they were not following the star of any abstraction. What, for instance, could have been more supremely, more "spiritually," empirical than the idea of making a Christian of that servant of the queen of Ethiopia whom Philip would never see again, after telling him of Jesus and baptizing him by the side of the road from Jerusalem to Gaza? This is perhaps an extreme case, but one could produce a whole series of cases in which the firmest general lines are variously interwoven with elements of chance and circumstance.

Thus, in the itinerant service of the word, a gradual division came, in particular, to operate between what was asked of the synagogue by way of support, and what was asked of the family. In the end, owing to rejection by the synagogue, it came to be the home which inherited the totality of the life of the Christian assembly—word, baptism, eucharist, good works, and so on. But the assembly was the *ekklesia* itself, invited and welcomed into the domestic sphere (*oikos ekklesias*). To that *ekklesia*, the home thus offered first of all the active support of hospitality and all that it involved, which was indeed a noteworthy contribution. For, with its hospitality, the home gave the *ekklesia* the assurance of a continuity in the local service of the word, at the same time as constituting a center from which all those—the apostles in particular—whose proper mission was still to carry the word beyond the assembly that already existed could work. Thus the domestic framework assured, both to the *ekklesia* and to the itinerant service of the word, not only stability and security, but also the flexibility and mobility which made it possible for the gospel to continue its advance.

In addition, through the ramifications of relationship, friendship, and service, as we see in that most illuminating example of the centurion Cornelius—and no doubt also through the natural ties of work and neighbourhood—the domestic framework from the first gave the itinerant service of the word and the *ekklesia* that developed from it, an extraordinarily strong and multiform link with the surrounding society. In this respect, it is no exaggeration to say that, on the institutional level, it was the context of the home, above all, which made it possible at that time for the gospel and the *ekklesia* to be the leaven in the lump.

However, the married state constituted a special problem for the itinerant servants of the word, and this must have been so most often and most urgently for those who were actually apostles. For the word, at its high point, was the "good news," and the "good news" must be proclaimed, for everything else depended on its being spread far and wide. Yet how could the "good news" possibly be told if the herald was not free to set out and tell it? More precisely: how could the "good news" be told with the fullness demanded by God's plan for all men if the herald himself was not so placed as to feel relatively free in his movements? Basically, then, it was the "good news" itself (*kerugma*), in its place in God's universal plan, which gave the herald (*kerux*) the yardstick he needed to measure how free he must be in its service (*diakonia*).[1]

How far, then, could such liberty allow for the married state? As a minimum, it required the ability to go away, for what kind of service could be rendered by a herald who could not leave home? But leaving is relative, and absences can be longer or shorter. The extreme is to leave for good. Jesus, as we know, asked his closest disciples to "leave all things" to "follow" him: house, father, mother, brothers, sisters, wife, children, goods, and occupations. Yet even this, despite its starkness, allowed for differing ways of doing it in the concrete which must have been less rigid than one would expect, for more than once we find the Twelve back in the context of their earlier lives, even after having "left all things" to "follow" Jesus.[2]

And it seems as if a similar pattern of behavior prevailed later on among the Twelve, and also among those who, following their example, dedicated themselves in various capacities to the itinerant service of the word. This, in any case, seems the likeliest interpretation of Paul's allusion, mentioned earlier, to the "other apostles," the "brothers of the Lord," and even Cephas himself being accompanied by a "wife" in fields of action often some distance away from their starting point. This also explains how Philip, having become an "evangelist" —which, whatever its precise meaning, indicates that he had passed beyond his earlier service of good works to the direct service of the

---

[1] In this sense 1 Cor 9 : 16–23; also, Acts 20 : 24; for an explicit connection of the double qualification of herald and apostle, see 1 Tim 2 : 7; 2 Tim 1 : 11.

[2] The cure of Peter's mother-in-law, "in the house of Simon and Andrew," in the presence of James and John (Mk 1 : 29–31); the meal in Levi-Matthew's house (Mk 2 : 15–17); the calming of the storm (Mk 5 : 35–41); the walking on the water (Mk 6 : 45–52); the fishing scene on the lake after the resurrection (Jn 21 : 1–8).

"good news"—finally settled at Caesarea with his four daughters (Acts 21 : 8–9). It is true that, on this occasion, Luke's account only mentions Philip's daughters, because there was a special interest in the fact of their being "prophetesses." But it is clear that Philip, the "evangelist," must in fact have taken his whole family with him to Caesarea.

We certainly have only very few details of this kind from which to judge of the situation as a whole. But those we have seem quite enough to show that there were, at the beginning, many and various ways of "leaving" one's old life to dedicate oneself to the itinerant service of the word. Besides, even the word "itinerant" cannot be made to suggest a single model, conceived once and for all in the abstract. In this respect, though there was one absolutely unchanging general purpose—that the "good news" must, according to the will of Jesus and the design of God, be carried to all, both near and far—one need only read the early documents with a modicum of care to realize that the varying circumstances of people, events, times, and places all made significant differences to the ways in which this general intention accepted by all was actually put into effect.

Nonetheless, the principle holds good that the "good news" must be better served by a greater measure of freedom on the part of the herald. Paul saw this with special clarity, while aware that his clarity of vision was not so much something to be proud of as a responsibility (1 Cor 9 : 15–23). Without any marriage tie, he gave himself wholly when the time came to the service of the gospel. Thus in his own way he took advantage of a situation that already existed, a situation which seemed to him personally a good thing in its own right (1 Cor 7 : 1, 7–8, 26–35). But, equally characteristically, he did not for a moment think, on that account, of forcing others to adopt his style of life, even under the veil of an indirect criticism which he might have made of them (1 Cor 9 : 5). Each could bring his own contribution to the common task, with a clear conscience. Paul knew that the gifts of God are many and varied (1 Cor 7 : 7), and he respected them, thus paying homage to the freedom of the God who gave them.

In any case, the number and variety of Paul's co-workers show, more clearly than anything he could have said, how profoundly genuine that respect was. Paul showed nothing but affection and gratitude to them all. Among them, we must remember, were his hosts, who had welcomed and protected him, who had offered him their homes as his safest, and ultimately, most effective, base of action, and who, during his longer visits, had provided him even with the means of exercising the trade by which he and his companions had their livelihood. There were also, of course, all those who had helped him in so many different ways in his actual service of the word, some for short times, others for years at a stretch, through travels and sufferings of all kinds.

Among those closest to Paul we find men and women whose family ties and situations are for the most part unknown to us. But we also find mention of married couples, and among them some of those to whom Paul feels he owes most in his service of the gospel. Nor does he admire them any the less: "Greet Prisca and Aquila, my fellow workers in Christ Jesus," he writes to the church in Rome, "who risked their necks for my life, to whom not only I, but all the churches of the Gentiles give thanks . . . Andronicus and Junias, my kinsmen and my fellow prisoners; they are [people] of note among the apostles, and they were in Christ before me."[3]

However, the assembly (*ekklesia*) which grew out of the welcome given to the message demanded, for the service of its own life, conditions in many ways different from those we find obtaining in the itinerant service of the word.

The framework of home and family still remained essential, of course; often indeed the assembly had but to re-form in the same place where the message had first formed it. The centurion Cornelius, who had invited his friends and relations to Peter's coming, could have been no less willing to receive the newly baptized in his home after the apostle's departure (Acts 10 : 24). Was not this, in fact, precisely what was needed to form the solid kernel of an *ekklesia*— those "called together" in the house of Cornelius? We do not know whether this was what happened, but this example is an excellent indication of how there could, within the domestic framework, be a concrete continuity between the message and the assembly it brought into being.

Nevertheless, obvious differences appeared between the conditions needed for the advance of the message and those needed for the life of the assembly. For the message was carried along by its own momen-

---

[3] Rom 16 : 3-4, 7; and in general, 16 : 1-15. See also 1 Cor 16 : 15: "You know that the household of Stephanas were the first converts in Achaia, and they have devoted themselves to the service of the saints; I urge you to be subject to such men and to every fellow-worker and labourer [as they are]." See, too, Philemon 1-2.

tum, so to speak, beyond the existing assembly, continually breaking through its barriers to give birth to new assemblies. It was the law of its nature, precisely as message, to keep crossing the frontiers of the already won whenever the possibility arose. It goes without saying that this law was primarily inscribed in the special service of the apostle, whose quality of "one sent" dictated at once both the style of his life and its deepest purpose. In this way, the distinctive demands of mobility and liberty were brought by the message itself to the very heart of the apostolic service.

But the *ekklesia* left behind by the message found that, precisely as an assembly, its law of existence was different. Its most specific and profound purpose in effect lay in the growth of the inner communion of its members through an exchanging of brotherly love, and a sharing in the hope of life in Jesus, the Christ and the Lord. And it was towards that exchange and that sharing, as the major sources of the *ekklesia*'s communion, that ultimately the mutual assistance, the local service of the word and the celebration of the "Lord's supper" were spontaneously directed.

Just as it is true to say, as we have seen, that the message in its quality of "good news" brought with it, from the very beginning of the apostolic service, a demand for mobility and freedom in all the branches of the itinerant service of the word, so it is equally true to say that, on the other hand, for the service of the assembly, brotherly communion required the quite different conditions of regularity and stability which were to be so characteristic of pastoral concern.

The metaphors of flock and shepherd were first developed in a consistent way in relation to the service of the assembly rather than to that of the apostolic message.[4] These images suggested above all closeness, attention, watchfulness, day-to-day care. And such was indeed the character of the service which the *ekklesia* could, and should, expect from those who were placed at its head, to preside over the assemblies of word and eucharist, and in a general way to ensure its cohesion and its progress in brotherly love and in hope.

The "shepherds" (Eph 4 : 11) of the "flock" were, however, more generally known as "presbyters" (Acts 11 : 30; 14 : 23; etc. or *episkopoi* (Phil 1 : 1); Acts 20 : 28; etc.). "Deacons," or servants, generally younger, were sometimes there to assist the presbyters-

[4] See Acts 20 : 28–9; Eph 4 : 11; 1 Pet 5 : 2–3. Compare, however, Jn 10 : 1–16; 21 : 16; Heb 13 : 20.

episkopoi in their service (1 Tim 3 : 8–13). But ultimately it was upon these last that the ordinary care of the *ekklesia* essentially fell.

What, then, were these presbyters-*episkopoi?* What kind of picture can we form of these first "shepherds" of the church? From our standpoint, the title of presbyter is of especial importance. *Presbuteros* is, indeed, a term laden with sociological associations. Hence, *presbuteros* at first contained what we may call far more "human substance" than the alternative *episkopos,* and it would seem also that it was *presbuteros* which was at first preferred in the Christian vocabulary.

Later, it is true, *episkopos* took over as designating the highest pastoral responsibility; and with time and the general development of institutions, it gained in substance. But we must beware of projecting back to the apostolic age what we can see in the second century. At the start, *episkopos* was a title closely related to the function; it was made to measure, to indicate in general a charge of "surveillance," or, better perhaps, of "superintendence." At the beginning, at least, that "superintendence" seems to have been understood simply in relation to the *ekklesia* itself; it was only later on that it came to be extended to the presbyters as well, then indicating a certain primacy of responsibility among them in the pastoral service.

Furthermore, neither *presbuteros* nor *episkopos* was, at the beginning, a title special to the internal organization of the Christian *ekklesia.* Both existed elsewhere, in the Jewish world and in the Greek; and both were thus simply adapted to suit the new reality of the *ekklesia.* We must, however, take care not to think that for this reason *presbuteros* and *episkopos* brought to their new function an equal fund of nuances and overtones from their ordinary human contexts.

As I have said, in this respect *presbuteros* was incomparably the richer. Before it had any religious overtones, *presbuteros* meant *elder.* Collectively, therefore, the *presbuteroi* were "the elders," as contrasted first of all with the *neoteroi* and the *neaniskoi,* who were the "young people" of the rising generation. In a narrower sociological term of reference, the *presbuteroi* were also the notables, and hence those liable to be given certain definite functions within the group. Thus the word brings us at once into the midst of a whole social reality involving the relationship between successive generations.

Not only this. When picturing to ourselves the pastoral service of the early church, we are all too inclined to forget that the quality and function of "presbyter" at that time had a strong sociological root in the family itself. We neglect the fact that in the group as a whole, the "presbyters" of the *ekklesia*, no less than the "elders" of the synagogue, belonged to what we may call the older generation of the "fathers." Now this fact of itself undoubtedly determined an image for everyone, and created a climate of thought in regard to the personal and social qualifications needed by "presbyters." As a general rule, we may say that this general image and climate of thought led everyone to see quite naturally in the "presbyter" a "father" who had already given proof of his human and social qualities in the running of his own "household."

Paul's comment seems in this respect absolutely characteristic. He wrote to Timothy (a presbyter, too, according to Tit 1 : 5–9) :

> A bishop (*episkopos*) must manage his own household well, keeping his children submissive and respectful in every way; for if a man does not know how to manage his own household, how can he care for God's church? [1 Tim 3 : 4–5.]

Fundamentally, the quality of "elder" ultimately leading to the function of "presbyter" thus appears as representing both chronological and social age. It was, first, the time of life by which one was supposed to have acquired, simply from the length of time spent in handling domestic responsibilities, a fund of experience and wisdom not possessed by the rising generation. But it was also the point of social integration by which one had become able to take part in councils, or called to share in running a group outside the family, such as the *ekklesia* itself, which had been born out of the gospel message.

In this way we can see how deeply marriage was involved in the pastoral service of the *ekklesia* in early times. Certainly, no one at that date ever envisaged such an abstract alternative as "celibacy-or-marriage," to be evaluated in the light of some hierarchy of the relative perfection of different "states of life." What was actually to be considered, with the presbyter-*episkopos*, as well as with the deacon, was the style of life—and that was something which could be judged from the facts, especially from the way in which the future servant of the assembly ran his own household. To see how this style of life would be carried over to another sphere was all the easier in that it was the household itself which provided the normal context for the assembly. It could be hoped that whoever ran his own home well would also be able to take care of "the church of God." A reasonable hope indeed. Who could ask more? And why should more be asked?

The home, on its side, offered the *ekklesia* an absolutely natural framework, and in addition an extraordinarily fruitful one, in which to unfold spaciously all the wealth of its own life: the service of the word, the service of the eucharist, the service of brotherly communion. Indirectly, it further offered the means of securing the continuity, dignity, and effectiveness of the pastoral service as a whole. The advantages in every way undoubtedly appeared great to the apostles themselves, as their message and instruction laid foundations in many places where churches were to be built up.

And great they were indeed, as experience was soon to show in the advance of the gospel. Thus it was with absolute serenity and joyful gratitude—and not as any mere concession to "human weakness" and the difficulties of making a beginning—that home and marriage were, both, and in a single sweep, profoundly integrated into the life of the apostolic church. The documents we still have bearing witness to the ideas and feelings of the time seem susceptible of no other interpretation.

Now it has been thought, and it still is quite generally thought, that Paul was making an exclusive pronouncement against those who had remarried when it came to choosing presbyters, bishops, and deacons. Yet if remarriage, of itself, was enough to incapacitate a man for the pastoral service, does not the shadow cast by Paul's statement ultimately lie upon marriage too? The distance between the two is short, indeed, and we know from history that marriage itself was not always presented in a very noble light in all those invitations to avoid remarriage of which we begin to find echoes from the middle of the second century onwards. It certainly looks as if Paul's thinking concerning the style of life which seemed to him best suited to the pastoral service of the assembly was imperceptibly leading that way:

A bishop (*episkopon*) must be above reproach, the husband of one wife (*mias gunaikos andra*), temperate, sensible, dignified, hospitable, an apt teacher (*didaktikon*). . . . Deacons likewise must be serious, not double-tongued (in their dealings with others), not addicted to much wine, not greedy for gain; . . . And let them also be tested first; then if they prove themselves blameless let them serve as deacons . . . Let deacons be the husband of one wife (*mias gunaikos andres*), and let them manage their children and their households well. [1 Tim 3 : 2, 8, 10, 12; compare Tit 1 : 6–9.]

On the whole, these recommendations are clear enough, even at this distance from the actual circumstances in which they were given. Behind a number of apparently very general qualifications, we can still discern those more precisely related to the life of the *ekklesia*: the many decisions to be taken for the good of each and all; the hospitality which was the only thing that made the meeting of the assembly possible at all at that time; the "instruction" whose special purpose was to mold for individuals and for the group the ideal of a life worthy of the gospel (Eph 4 : 1); the multitude of relationships of all kinds through which the *ekklesia* took concrete form in its meetings; the organizing of community meals, the service and development of good works, and so on. We can easily imagine, further, the more or less serious harm that would be done to the service of the assembly by this or that fault in a bishop or deacon.

One absolutely certain point—and, in the matter we are dealing with, a decisive one—is that certain relatively well-defined qualities and aptitudes were sought in those responsible for pastoral service not for their own sake, but for their usefulness, convenience, and adaptation to the needs of the time. It was a completely concrete way of thinking, clearly supported by actual experience.

One may, however, still hesitate in interpreting the meaning to be attached to one particular qualification required of candidates. Whatever meaning we arrive at, it is a qualification of special interest to our study. We cannot avoid examining the problem here, especially since, in spite of everything, the pastoral tradition of the church, from at least the end of the second century, has found in Paul's phrase one of its clearest signposts. The *episkopos*, the presbyter, and the deacon —said Paul—must be *mias gunaikos andres*. What did he mean? In itself, the literal translation of the three words is quite simple: *husband of a single wife*. But is it not in fact too simple? Should we not perhaps look to see whether there is some less obvious allusion underlying it?

At a first glance the phrase would seem to forbid polygamy. But that is in every sense excluded in advance for a Christian community, and would thus make Paul's recommendation lose all its point. Some have therefore suggested a reference to conjugal fidelity. In that case

Paul would be meaning that candidates for the pastoral service must be known to be faithful to their wife. But if that is all he meant, why did he say it so obscurely? And on three separate occasions? This meaning would make his phrase a bit strange, in any case. Once more, one suspects that it refers to something else.

Now there is of course a third interpretation, which by far the greatest number of people prefer, and which seems to present itself here. Paul must be alluding to remarriage, and in that sense is demanding that the *episkopos*, presbyter, and deacon have been "husbands" of only "one wife." We must recognize that this solution has, first of all, the incontestable merit of doing full justice to the Greek. Furthermore, in the context of one evaluation of marriage at least, a demand thus expressed might at first sight take a most natural place among Paul's recommendations as a whole.

Nevertheless, on reflection, one wonders whether making remarriage the key to interpreting the phrase does not also come up against one fatal obstacle, given the context—which is actually concerned only with *present* aptitudes, or inaptitudes. It enumerates the qualities that would be a help in the service of the *ekklesia*, and the defects which might in the end, to a greater or lesser extent, compromise that service. But a remarriage is neither an inaptitude nor a defect; it is a domestic event to be judged in the light of circumstances (1 Cor 7 : 8–9, 15, 39,; 1 Tim 5 : 14). It may be urged against this that in Paul's thinking, it was precisely the remarriage which created the inaptitude; but it is surely just this which has to be proved in the first place. And that no one has succeeded in doing.

In the last analysis, it is hard to see how such a man as Paul, with his firm Jewish traditions (1 Tim 4 : 1–6), could have given himself over to calculating the suitability or otherwise of a possible previous remarriage on the part of the *episkopoi*, presbyters, and deacons of the *ekklesia*.[5] It is all the harder to imagine his taking such a stand since, when dealing with the situation of widows, he does not seem to have displayed the same concern in regard to widowers—for the obviously excellent reason that in that time and place, the actual chances of a prolonged widowhood, or ultimate remarriage, were in all respects most unequal for the two sexes.

Finally, since the clause *mias gunaikos anèr* is used in each instance without the smallest intention that one can see of offering any expla-

[5] Compare 1 Tim 5 : 9 on the enrolling of widows.

nation in the context, and in two out of the three cases is directly alongside such a familiar subject as running a household well (1 Tim 3 : 12; Tit 1 : 6), it would seem unlikely that we can only find Paul's meaning somewhere in the distant byways of the supposed unsuitable-ness of a possible—and perhaps already long-standing—remarriage on the part of candidates for the pastoral service of the assembly. The true sense of Paul's phrase must surely lie much nearer to hand.

It seems to me, in spite of everything that has been said about it, that the literary make-up of the phrase really gives us an obvious clue to the meaning. If I said of someone that he was a "man of one book," no one would take the expression literally. On the contrary, everyone would understand this as referring to his behavior and atti-tude—not to the number of books he has. If I say of a man of action that he has been all his life a "man of one idea," or if I say of a friend on whose loyalty I can always depend that he is a "man of his word," everyone at once understands that in the first case I am speaking of a whole lifetime spent in carrying out a great project, and in the second, of a fidelity which cannot be shaken from a promise once given.

Similarly, it is not hard to go on to see that the "husband of one wife" could simply mean a husband "undividedly attached to his wife"—which is, in fact, the sense which seems best to fit the context. If we follow the general trend of Paul's instruction, we soon realize that he is not concerned here with an event in a man's past life which suddenly appears in the present as an unexpected obstacle to the service of the assembly (as remarriage would be), but rather with a present attitude which would naturally appear among the qualifica-tions required for the pastoral service of the *ekklesia*.

Now that is precisely what Paul's phrase would be if one takes it to mean a husband "undividedly attached to his wife." In short, what Paul is asking here is that the servants of the assembly begin by giving all the signs of a harmonious and stable marriage. Whether it be their first marriage or their second does not matter for the moment. That is not the point. In the same strain, Paul then goes on to demand that the servants of the *ekklesia* should first of all show that they are well able to run their own household. In each case, what is sought is an assurance that the pastoral service itself will be performed with dig-nity and efficiency. This is straightforward, realistic, and consistent.[6]

---

[6] The interpretation put forward here is substantially the one favored long ago by Theodore of Mopsuestia (*Commentary on the epistles of Paul: 1 Tim 3 : 2* [ed. Swete II, 99–108]).

If further confirmation is needed, this interpretation is also supported by the parallelism of *monandros* (Latin: *univira*[7]="wife of one husband") and *mias gunaikos aner* (="husband of one wife"). As a general rule, *monandros* and *univira* are terms of praise in both Jewish and pagan inscriptions of the time. In any hypothesis, the dead wife who is praised as having been *monandros*, or *univira*, is certainly not being congratulated on never having contracted a second marriage —as is especially clear in those cases in which the praise has been given by the surviving husband, but, as far as one can possibly see, for having been wholeheartedly attached to her husband.[7] No other interpretation is possible.

It would seem, then, that this must also be the sense of the Pauline phrase *mias gunaikos aner*: "husband of one wife," or in other words "undividedly attached to his wife." If that is indeed what it means, the particular question of remarriage becomes simply beside the point. We must look elsewhere to see what Paul thought about that.

Having required that the *episkopos* be "above reproach, undividedly attached to his wife, temperate, sensible, and dignified," Paul considers it important also that he be *philoxenos* ("hospitable").[8] It has generally been understood that this hospitality was mainly to be in regard to Christians on their travels, whether simply moving from place to place, or actually on missions. And there can be no doubt that Paul, in organizing the service of the assembly, would not have forgotten the valuable witness of brotherly communion which hospitality of that kind must always give. Through the generous kindness of their hosts as they travelled, the churches could in fact recognize in a tangible form the bonds linking them together in one hope and one love.

But it does not appear that this hospitality, which was after all only occasional, was in the forefront of Paul's mind in this instance. Nor was it the special responsibility of the *episkopoi* or presbyters—on the contrary, we know that it was a duty laid upon all Christians.[9] The recommendations Paul gives, taken as a whole, would in fact rather lead us to suppose that what he was primarily thinking of here was *pastoral hospitality*. It may be further added that the very structure of the pastoral service of the *ekklesia* at that time required it.

For we must not forget that, at that date, the assembly which

---

[7] Compare 1 Tim 5 : 9: *Henos andros gune*, which has the same sense.
[8] Tim 3 : 2. We find the same thing recommended for presbyters, Tit 1 : 8.
[9] See Rom 12 : 13; 1 Tim 5 : 10; Heb 13 : 2; 1 Pe 4 : 9; 3 Jn 5–8.

constituted the *ekklesia* was, literally, invited and welcomed in the ordinary setting of domestic hospitality. This meant, first of all, that one or other of the Christians whose home was available agreed to receive the assembly in it.[10] But it also meant that the host was one of the servants of the assembly in the strict sense: *episkopoi* (or pres-byters) and deacons actually welcomed the *ekklesia* wherever it was arranged for it to meet. That welcome, directly built into ordinary hospitality, and adopting many of its customs, was—after the invita-tion and whatever other useful preliminary steps might be indicated by the circumstances—the first pastoral act of the *episkopoi* or pres-byters, assisted by their deacons, in regard to the assembly.

Nor can we doubt that this pastoral welcome was one of the most important functions in the service of the *ekklesia*, for it was effectively this which actually re-formed the *ekklesia* every time it assembled to hear the word, or renew the "Lord's supper," or both. Thus it was in large measure upon the quality of the pastoral welcome within the assembly that its whole internal order and cohesion directly depended. Similarly, at every gathering, it was primarily the pastoral welcome which, in the concrete, re-created the bonds of Christian brotherhood around the word and the eucharist. At the beginning, therefore, it was that welcome which made the "communion" of the *ekklesia*; without it, it would not have been long before everything else ground to a helpless halt.

It also brought one of the major contributions to the work of widening out the *ekklesia*. It was largely thanks to it, in effect, that the *ekklesia* could always remain so open to the rest of the world, attract-ing sympathetic interest, and winning new believers in the gospel. In this way, the pastoral welcome had a most important "apostolic" value. From within the existing assembly, it paved the way for the message itself. It was certainly in considerable part to the pastoral welcome for which the assembly provided the occasion, that the gos-pel owed its rapid and extraordinary penetration into the mass of the urban population of the time.

We are looking back from a great distance. From where we are it is almost impossible for most of us to suspect even the existence of these things. Yet they did exist, and their value in advancing the hope of the gospel was outstanding, if not irreplaceable. We are still able to read the texts which give evidence of their magnificence and their vitality,

[10] Rom 16 : 5 (Prisca and Aquila); 1 Cor 16 : 19 (the same); Col 4 : 15 (Nymphas); Philemon 2 (Philemon and Apphia).

but it is not very easy for us to see the exact form they took. All kinds of images, more or less conventional, more or less anachronistic, fill the gap between things as they are now and the primitive pastoral service. Different levels merge, and all the riches we might get from a tradition which could still be creative get lost on the way.

Thus we read quite plainly that Paul wanted to see the *ekklesia* headed by "hospitable" men—in other words, men endowed with the qualities that make for genuine hospitality (1 Tim 3 : 2–3; Tit 1 : 7–9). But do we understand what we read? Hospitality, yes, we say—and we think at once of travellers. The direct link between that "hospitality" and both the original domestic context of the assembly and the effective exercise of the primitive pastoral service as a whole, escapes us, and we go on to other matters.

Yet this style of pastoral service did not exist merely once; it lasted for a long time. We can even say, without risk of serious error, that its activity made itself felt for more than two centuries without any major changes of form. Therefore, to conclude this long analysis, in which the early documents have so often brought marriage and the home before us, I cannot do better than to produce here one last witness of the pastoral hospitality of old. It dates from around the middle of the third century. Its direct horizon was probably that of Syria. In essentials, the pastoral customs it shows go back much earlier than the actual composing of the work; indeed, in their main points, they could be a fairly faithful reflection of the state of things in earliest times. There is, too, good reason to think that the customs of Syria were at that time closely related to what was generally done throughout the church.

True, in the third century the place of assembly was no longer, as a general rule, the home of one of the members of the *ekklesia*. Thus it was not, strictly speaking, a "home." It was in most cases a former home now more or less rearranged, altered, and sometimes enlarged, to fit the special needs of the Christian assembly. In consequence, the "church," as it was by then beginning to be called, while keeping the general appearance of a genuine *domus ecclesiae*, or *oikos ekklesias*, had in fact become a fixed meeting place, and at least in theory, always available and therefore no longer needing in itself the many and varied personal attentions which went to make up the earlier pastoral hospitality. It is, however, worth noting, that in addition to the space allowed for the assembly, the "church" of those days was tending more and more to include extra rooms in which to accommodate a greater or smaller proportion of those involved in pastoral service: bishop, priests, and deacons. In general, however, the lectors and other helpers continued to live among the general population.

Given the tremendous transformations that had come about in the physical setting of the assembly, it is all the more remarkable to find to what extent pastoral hospitality still remained alive and significant in the awareness of the customs of the church. The anonymous author of the *Didascalia apostolorum* devotes a long time to developing it in the instructions he gives to the bishops of his time. The picture he gives for the purpose is certainly, by the very nature of the literary form he is using, idealized; what he presents is more in the nature of a program. But, if it is to have any chance of actually being carried out, that program must obviously propose a pastoral way of life that would be still possible to most people. Thus, through the ideal the author is aiming at, we get glimpses of a situation which must have been fairly familiar to most of his contemporaries. I trust I shall be excused for quoting almost the whole passage here—for its wealth of detail, its inspiration, and not least for its genuine and simple beauty:

> And you the bishops, be not hard, not tyrannical, nor wrathful, and be not rough with the people of God which is delivered into your hands. And destroy not the Lord's house nor scatter his people; but convert all, that you may be helpers with God; and gather the faithful with much meekness and long-suffering and patience, and without anger, and with doctrine and exhortation, as ministers of the kingdom everlasting.
>
> And in your congregations in the holy churches hold your assemblies with all decent order, and appoint the places for the brethren with care and gravity. And for the presbyters let there be assigned a place in the eastern part of the house; and let the bishop's throne be set in their midst, and let the presbyters sit with him. And again, let the lay men sit in another part of the house toward the east. For so it should be, that in the eastern part of the house the presbyters sit with the bishops, and next the lay men, and then the women; that when you stand up to pray, the rulers may stand first, and after them the lay men, and then the women also. For it is required that you pray toward the east, as knowing that which is written: *Give ye glory to God, who rideth upon the heaven of heavens toward the east.* [Ps 68 : 24.]
>
> But of the deacons let one stand always by the oblations of the Eucharist; and let another stand without by the door and observe them that enter. But later, at the time of the oblation, let them minister together in the church. And if any one be found sitting out of his place,

let the deacon who is within reprove him and make him to rise up and sit in a place that is meet for him. For our Lord likened the church to a fold; for as we see the dumb animals, oxen and sheep and goats, lie down and rise up, and feed and chew the cud, according to their families, and none of them separate itself from its kind; and (see) the wild beasts also severally range with their like upon the mountains; so likewise in the church ought those who are young to sit apart, if there be room, and if not to stand up; and those who are advanced in years to sit apart. And let the children stand on one side, or let their fathers and mothers take them to them; and let them stand up. And let the young girls also sit apart; but if there be no room, let them stand up behind the women. And let the young women who are married and have children stand apart, and the aged women and widows sit apart. And let the deacon see that each of them on entering goes to his place, that no one may sit out of his place. And let the deacon also see that no one whispers, or falls asleep, or laughs, or makes signs. For so it should be, that with decency and decorum they watch in the church, with ears attentive to the word of the Lord.

But if any brother or sister come from another congregation, let the deacon question her and learn whether she is married, or again whether she is a widow (who is) a believer; and whether she is a daughter of the church, or belongs perchance to one of the heresies; and then let him conduct her and set her in a place that is suitable for her. But if a presbyter should come from another congregation, do you the presbyters receive him with fellowship into your place. And if it be a bishop, let him sit with the bishop; and let him accord him the honor of his rank, even as himself. And do thou, O bishop, invite him to discourse to thy people; for the exhortation and admonition of strangers is very profitable, especially as it is written: *There is no prophet that is acceptable in his own place* [cf. Mt 13 : 57, and parallels]. And when you offer the oblation, let him speak. But if he is wise and gives the honor to thee, and is unwilling to offer, at least let him speak over the cup.

But if, as you are sitting, some one else should come, whether a man or a woman, who has some worldly honor, either of the same district or of another congregation; thou, O bishop, if thou art speaking the word of God, or hearing, or reading, shalt not respect persons and leave the ministry of thy word and appoint them a place; but do thou remain still as thou art and not interrupt thy word, and let the brethren themselves receive them. But if, while younger men or women sit, an older man or woman should rise and give up their place, do thou, O deacon, scan those who sit, and see which man or woman of them is younger than the rest, and make them stand up, and cause him to sit who had risen and given up his place; and let him whom thou hast caused to stand up, lead away and make him to stand behind his neighbors: that others also may be trained and learn to give place to those more honorable than themselves. But if a poor man or woman should come, whether of the same district or of another congregation, and especially if they are stricken in years, and there be no place for such, do thou, O bishop, with all thy heart provide a place for them, even if thou have to sit upon the ground; that thou be not as one who respects the persons of men, but that thy ministry may be acceptable with God.[11]

[11] *Didascalia Apostolorum,* 12 (trans. and ed. Connolly, 119–24).

Conclusion

Some of the details brought to light in our analysis call, in conclusion, for a certain number of more general observations, mainly concerned with the way in which the service of the word and the service of the assembly were first envisaged. For there seems in fact to have been, both with Jesus and his immediate disciples, a perfectly recognizable point of view spontaneously adopted by them all.

In this respect, what must be noted first of all is that they were from the start unhesitatingly concerned with *styles of life* whose main lines were determined by the specific needs of all the various functions that developed, rather than with *states of life* dictated from above and fixed once and for all by a hierarchy of degrees of perfection in man's relationship with God and his neighbor. We many say, therefore, that there were as many styles of life as there were distinct functions, and as many distinct functions as there were recognized needs and talents to satisfy them, whether relating to the service of the word, or of the *ekklesia*. In the last analysis, then, it was in every case the evident needs and the available talents which dictated how the style of life adapted to the function and service required of it.

As was natural, these general conditions gave birth to a rapid and extremely rich diversification, in both styles of action and styles of life, within the one service of the hope of the gospel, in which all were united in the pursuit of a single goal. The rule seemed to be, and indeed, was, one of extreme flexibility. But it is quite clear that this flexibility was not sought for its own sake as some ideal rule favored by some abstract theory of evangelical activity. Rather was it the result, in the first place, of a general acceptance of concrete situations, and, in the second, of a spontaneous conviction that God's plan was as all-embracing as his gifts were many and varied.

From this standpoint, Jesus' own example was itself quite decisive. His initial message had represented a certain style of activity, which naturally came to sustain a style of life appropriate to it. That style of activity and style of life were inspired, though in the freest sense, by the already old-established image of the prophet, the herald of Yahweh, whose task was to spread widely and rapidly the "good news" from God of a hope soon to be made manifest.

The disciples who were first drawn into close friendship with Jesus could hardly fail to perceive the profound differences introduced into his earlier style of activity and style of life by the mere fact of the changeover from message to instruction. Those differences were certainly obvious enough. Having presented himself as a prophet, sent by God to announce to the people the "good news" of the forthcoming fulfillment of the hope promised of old, Jesus became the master who sat still, who surrounded himself with dedicated disciples who "followed" him when he journeyed, and also welcomed the more or less chance groups of listeners who formed around him, in order slowly and patiently to lift the veil that, almost by force of circumstances, had come to cover the first message.

Had the disciples needed further illustration, the first sending of them, actually in the lifetime of Jesus, would have been enough to make clear the natures of the instruction and of the message respectively, both from the point of view of style of life and from that of style of activity. For at that point, the disciples had been "following" Jesus for some time, and were well aware of how Jesus' instruction determined his life as a master dedicated to disclosing now in depth the sense and scope of his initial message.

What their mission did for the disciples, on this occasion, was to enable them to live the experience of spreading a message similar in every way to the initial message of Jesus himself. As a result of this, had they failed to realize it before, the disciples would know from then on at least what form of action the message represented, and what form of life would be normally suited to it. Fortunately, the gospel tradition has preserved a memory for us not only of the way in which Jesus at that time envisaged the disciples' mission, but also of the main recommendations he thought it useful to make to them in the circumstances to prepare them for it.

As one might have expected, the apostolic age presents a considerably more complex picture. Nonetheless, its development follows the main lines of Jesus' thought and activity. Thus we find the two major forms of the word, message and instruction, entering now upon a long process of inner differentiation, under the combined impact of individual talents and new situations arising out of the advance of the gospel. The "kerygmatic discourse" which appeared at this time, of which we can get a fairly good notion from reading Acts, was already far removed, in point of form, from the initial message of Jesus. Nor were the changes taking place in the literary forms of the instruction any less remarkable. In addition, at this period, new forms began to appear in the service of the word, and on these the extent of our information varies. We see them chiefly in relation to the individual gifts of the different evangelists, prophets, and doctors.

Changes in literary form generally indicate here parallel changes in style of activity. This, in its turn, molds a style of life to fit it to the varying needs recognized in concrete situations. In this way, we can certainly say that an itinerant service of the word existed at that time. But to give it this blanket description must not lay us open to the mistake of imagining the style of life of those involved as being always a uniform one, for that was far from being the case. Within the general framework of a certain freedom of movement which they all had, living conditions of very varied kinds were considered quite normal and legitimate.

When circumstances led him to stay anywhere for long, Paul would take up work to support himself. But there were others of a different opinion, who preferred to depend more completely on hospitality. Despite the small amount of information we have, it seems that a similar kind of diversity prevailed in regard to domestic situations as well. It is certainly glorious to see a man of Paul's quality, whose circumstances allow of complete personal liberty, taking advantage of that liberty to serve the gospel. But we must be careful not to confuse our categories: the quality and the liberty are two distinct things. And others, who were faced with more complex family situations, or who had begun by seeing marriage itself in a more favorable light, adopted a quite different line of conduct. Their doing so did not mean that having "left all things" they were in any sense thinking better of it, or looking back. It meant simply that ultimately they judged everything, as Jesus himself had, in the light of what was suitable and needful in the concrete conditions of their service, with due allowance for the situation that already existed, according to the higher rules of justice and love.

From our point of view, however, it is when we come to compare the itinerant service of the word with the service of the *ekklesia* that we discover the most significant feature of all. These were, in effect, two situations, and two quite distinct sets of conditions. The word demanded of the messenger of the gospel a mobility which could not but loosen the family tie. Thus if at that time there were a service which might, of its nature, suggest celibacy to those who became responsible for it, it was incontestably the apostolic service of the message, a vital form of the total service of the word.

Now when the birth of the *ekklesia* made it desirable to provide a special service to look after it, there was no question of making some haphazard adaptation of the apostolic service: absolutely new functions were created, and special responsibility for them was assumed by a quite different lot of people. Once again, the inner structure of the service was judged in the light of actual situations as these brought new needs to light.

Thus was born the "pastoral" service. This image, a most telling one in that time and place, served of itself to stress the basic intention that lay behind the creation of the service. Unlike the message, the *ekklesia* demanded stability and regularity. And where, under the circumstances, could one hope to find that stability and regularity present together with more other advantages than in the context of the home—both as a meeting place for the assembly, and as a welcome background of family support for those bearing the responsibilities of the *ekklesia*? Thus in fact it came about that the original service of the *ekklesia*, far from beginning by suggesting any weakening of the family structures into which it entered—which would in any case have been very poor strategy!—visibly sought, on the contrary, the support of everything most solid and permanent that those structures could offer it.

In this respect, the Pauline recommendations as to the choice of *episkopoi*, presbyters, and deacons seem to me absolutely unambiguous. They make it clear that in Paul's view, the framework of a home, with its living mesh of human relationships, with its wonderfully rich and strong customs of hospitality along with the marriage which constituted its essential and permanent reality, was a veritable education in the governing and serving of small groups, and at that time represented the only concrete and tangible possibility for the *ekklesia*—for the local service of the word, for the frequent service of the eucharist, and for the continual service of fraternal charity in all its various forms.

However, two and a half centuries later, the documents begin to give equally clear indications that the balance of the early days was on the point of being overthrown—or was even perhaps overthrown already—in every area of the ecclesial domain. What had happened? A great many things, obviously, which went far deeper than pastoral institutions, right down to the deepest layers of the Christian consciousness. And it is here, it seems to me, that the obligation to conjugal continence enshrined in canon 33 of the Council of Elvira, which I analyzed at the beginning, finally finds its meaning. For the moment, anyhow, we can limit ourselves to this one piece of evidence, for it contains the whole essence of what directly concerns our purpose.

First of all, then, the ruling of Elvira implicitly contains one point of capital importance: from then on, as had indeed been the case for some time beforehand, it was no longer to be the service of the word which, of its nature, especially in the dominant form of the message, gave the invitation to "leave all things"—home, father, mother, brothers, sisters, wife, and children—as was the case in apostolic times, but the pastoral service of the *ekklesia* itself—or, to be more precise, not the pastoral service of the *ekklesia* in general, but the specific service of the *sacramenta*, and thus, supremely, the service (*ministerium*) of the eucharist. Secondly, that same ruling also implicitly contains another point, directly related to the first and no less important: from then on, the church's reflection on the structures of its pastoral service was to turn more and more from a consideration of *styles of life*, determined at the actual level of realities by the changing conditions of the services involved, to a preferential consideration of *states of life*, prescribed from above by the ideally unchanging conditions of Christian perfection. The rest we know from history. For this twofold change—whose novelty in relation to the prevailing state of things in the apostolic generation we are now in a position to recognize —was to have incalculable consequences for centuries, right down to our own time.

I do not want to enter here into such detailed explanations that we are led away from our point. However, one or two things do call for special comment. The first concerns the influence of asceticism—and, later, of monasticism—on the pastoral service of the church. Obviously, all historians take this into consideration—indeed, one could hardly fail to recognize it. However, the type of reflection normally suggested to us on this subject is not always on a really fundamental level. It seems to me that the most important contribution of asceticism and monasticism has been precisely to have brought, first into pastoral thinking, and then into the actual structures of the service of the *ekklesia*, their own distinctive and original idea of a certain ideal "state" of Christian "perfection." Owing to the historical circumstances in which it was presented, that idea was in fact endowed from the very first with a spiritual aura that was quite enough to assure it a tremendous force of persuasion. It gradually became so universally present, in all the branches and under all the aspects of the church's pastoral service, that it is very hard indeed for us today to imagine any other state of affairs. And yet things were once very different, and if, in the order of the structures of pastoral service, a certain freedom of movement and of direction has been lost, it is only because we have allowed it to be.

A second, and more physical, factor is also involved—a factor whose action became deeply felt only very gradually, affecting both the theory and the structures of pastoral service. I mean the place of the liturgical assembly. From the moment when the place of assembly stopped being dictated by chance of circumstances,[1] all kinds of changes, involving the style of meetings, the habits of the pastors, and even the deepest feelings of the community itself, could now take place almost imperceptibly. Thus it became possible to hold meetings

---

[1] See the *Acta* of Justin Martyr (c. AD 165): "The prefect asked in what place the Christians assembled. Each, replied Justin, goes to the place of his choice, according to what is possible" (2). Compare Hippolytus, *Apostolic Tradition*, (c. AD 215): "When they awake and rise, let the faithful, before setting about their occupations, pray to God, and only then do they give themselves to their work. But if there is [service of the] word with instruction, let them give preference to that: let them go to hear the word of God to give strength to their souls. One should be in haste to go to the *ekklesia* where the Spirit abounds" (31–5); "Let the deacons and priests meet together every day in the place indicated by the bishop. Let deacons, especially, never fail to meet every day, unless sickness prevents them. Then, when they have had their meeting together, let them instruct"—or, "let them go to instruct"—"those [of the faithful] who are at the *ekklesia*. And after having prayed, let each go about his business" (33–9).

with greater regularity; buildings could be arranged in such a way as to increase the size of the groups meeting there. The (already rather marked) shift away from the original family framework heralded a slow but sure dissolution of the old customs of pastoral hospitality, and their eventual replacement by other more limited, more impersonal forms of welcome, more like those normally used in public meeting places. Then too, once in a fixed spot, the place of assembly itself could evoke in the minds of the faithful and their pastors the aura which generally attached to places of worship—the character of sacredness.

This in itself was a huge change, yet it still did not exhaust the possibilities of transformation involved in making the place of assembly a fixed one. For such an arrangement was, in fact, a direct invitation to all those chiefly responsible for the service of the *ekklesia* to group themselves closely round the place where the assembly was held. Thus, suddenly, an effective opening spontaneously appeared for the gradual establishment of a higher degree of organization in the pastoral service, and to that extent a favorable occasion for strengthening the "hierachization" of local power and functions. As we have seen, the *domus ecclesiae* of the third century gradually ceased to be simply a collection of rooms used for worship, and became a complexus that linked worship and domicile in such a way that the leading functionaries of the *ekklesia* lived near each other, and all relatively near the places where their service was carried out. Later, as the *domus ecclesiae* came to be replaced by the basilica, that same tendency was to be carried further still.

At the point when the ideal of the "state" of perfection—which had grown in all essentials out of asceticism and monasticism—began to be introduced into the service of the *ekklesia*, there existed just the conditions needed to foster it—in the actual arrangement of the locale, and the desire for pastoral regrouping that had already taken root. It was but a short step to the explicit ideal of the "common life" (*vita communis* coming to inform from within the pastoral service itself. For the West, we need only recall here the examples of Eusebius of Vercellae in Italy, Martin of Tours in Gaul, and—greatest of all—Augustine of Hippo in Africa.

However important it may have been, however, the twofold factor of the development of the monastic ideal, and the desire for a pastoral regrouping, is still not an adequate explanation of how such a ruling as that of Elvira could impose continence as a strict obligation upon all married bishops, priests, and deacons, from the moment of their taking up their respective functions in the service of the *ekklesia*. The monastic ideal was still a personal option; nor did the pastoral regrouping around the place of assembly in itself imply either the "common life" properly so-called, or any obligation to married continence. There was in fact another factor involved—and it was the truly decisive one.

This factor, as we know, was the encounter—within the pastoral consciousness itself—of the perception of the impure and the perception of the sacred, with the first appearing in the murkiest light in the form of the exercise of sexuality, and the second in the brightest as the service of the *sacramenta*. And it is evident that such an encounter must from the first have been one essentially of conflict. The pastoral desire to honour the *sacramenta* eventually reached such a point as to allow for only one possibility: the total exclusion of the exercise of sexuality, for by then it was hard to see how it could ever be freed from the shame of at least some degree of uncleanness.[2] Thus it would seem that only a thoroughgoing law of continence, imposed on all married clerics engaged in the direct service of the *sacramenta*, could provide a fitting disposition. Such was the Elvira ruling.

Having reached this point, it will be now more useful for us to leave Elvira and look at the question from another point of view.

---

[2] Minutius Felix, *Octavius*: "The wish for incest is so far from our minds [i.e., we Christians], that even honourable relations inspire shame among many of us" (31, 5); Ambrose, *Exhortatio virginitatis*: "Now indeed (since Adam has sinned, and Eve been stung by the serpent with the poison of lubricity), even though marriage be good, it still brings with it such things that make even married couples blush together" (6, 36); Jerome, *Adversus Iovinianum*: "Faced with [or, "in the presence of"] the purity of Christ's body, all sexual union is impure" (*omnis coitus immundus*) (1, 20). The immediate context of this last quotation calls to mind the episode of David with Ahimelek, in 1 Sam 21 : 2–7—the type of the encounter of pure and impure with the sacred, which Jerome here applies to the eucharist. The loaves of oblation are compared with the body of Christ; those who had come straight from the beds of their wives could not eat of them. How much more then, he says, must we feel that this applies to us. For "faced with the purity of Christ's body, all sexual union is impure."

Part Two

YESTERDAY, TODAY, AND TOMORROW

5

The Sacralization of the Pastoral Service and the Origins of the Law of Ecclesiastical Celibacy

Recruitment for the priesthood, priestly formation, priestly ministry, priestly spirituality, episcopal consecration, hierarchy—this phraseology, of which one could give many other examples, is familiar enough to us today. So familiar is it, in fact, that we should be almost unable to speak of the pastoral service without making use of it.

In this regard, even otherwise careful historians sometimes naively let themselves be caught in the trap of anachronism. They will, for instance, explain to us, with no further qualification, that Clement of Rome used the "ancient [i.e. Aaronic] priesthood" as a figure of the "Christian priesthood"—which does not just simplify, but actually misconstrues, Clement's thought.[1] Or, again, quoting Rom 15 : 16, in

---

[1] Clement of Rome, 1 *Corinthians*, especially 40–44. A positive picture of the old Levitical order by no means implies in itself that the author is picturing the pastoral service of the church as a new "priesthood." The standpoint of the epistle is that of justice, reconciliation, and peace, and—in a more general way—of regulating the life of the community in Corinth in a satisfactory way. It was in this connection that Clement's exhortation made use of the example given in olden days by the Aaronic priesthood. If the institutions of old, he explains, foreshadowed so long ago an admirable ordering of worship, how much more should we now try to observe the rule of order in all things, as our surest guarantee of charity and peace. Furthermore, how can we hope to please God if we allow the rule of division and injustice to be established among us?

It is important also to note that in Clement's writings, *leitourgein, leitourgia,* and *leitourgos* only carry a ceremonial and sacral meaning when they refer to the Levitical priesthood (32 : 2; 40 : 5; 41 : 2; except perhaps in 41 : 1). The author in fact returns to the more general sense of a "service" of the community every time he deals with the responsibility of presbyter-bishops towards their

77

which Paul speaks of the grace he has been given in his capacity as "servant," as "a minister (*leitourgon*) of Christ Jesus to the Gentiles," the mission of announcing "the gospel of God" having been conferred on him as one administering a "priestly service" (*hierourgounta*), in order to make the Gentiles an "offering" (*prosphora*) acceptable to God, "sanctified (*hegiasmene*) by the Holy Spirit," they will cheerfully pass from the level of occasional metaphor to that of full reality.[2] Thus we are invited simply to understand that Paul himself conceived "the apostolic ministry of the preaching of the gospel" as a "priestly function." Yet it is clear that such an interpretation, in the absolute form in which it is presented, goes much further than the intention of the original text.

What we must say, unhesitatingly and unambiguously, is that our "priestly" phraseology, though very old, is still not primitive. It has undergone a development; it has a history. The history, especially, is of the utmost importance for our present situation and some of our present difficulties. It touches very closely, in particular, upon the question of "clerical celibacy"; and it is this point that I want to examine briefly now. It seems to me that up to the present it has not been given the attention it deserves.

It is vital first of all to point out that none of the terms used at the beginning to designate the "service" of the "gospel" or of the *ekklesia* was taken over from the sacral world of the Jews: *apostolos, euagge-*

"flock," or with the "function" each has in the good ordering of the *ekklesia* (8 : 1; 41 : 1; 44 : 2, 3, 6; compare 9 : 2, 4; 20 : 10; 36 : 3; *hierateuein*, associated once only with *leitourgein*, 43 : 4, refers to the Levitical priesthood). We may note, similarly, that Clement never used the sacral term *hiereis* to designate the presbyter-bishops. On the contrary, *hiereis* is used once for the "priest" of the Egyptian religion (25 : 5) and twice for the "priests" of the Levitical order (32 : 2; 40 : 5). And *arkhiéreus* is used twice for the Levitical "high priest" (40 : 5; 41 : 2), and three times for Jesus himself in his state of glory with the Father (36 : 1; 61 : 3; 64). It is also significant, on the other hand, that Jesus' "priesthood" here seems to be placed in the line of the "order of Aaron" rather than in any prolonging of the "order of Melchizedek" (this latter is not named; 32 : 2 mentions Levi with such evident favour that he appears to have priority over Judah; Clement may be further suggesting a Levitical descent for Jesus; compare Heb 7 : 1–28).

[2] The accusative *to euaggelion tou theou*, object of the action indicated by *hierourgounta*, is enough to show that this latter term is being used metaphorically. The metaphor is obviously suggested here by a slight shift in the general sense of *leitourgon* in the clause of the preceding sentence (compare Rom 1 : 9: "God . . . whom I serve (*latreuo*) with my spirit" by proclaiming "the gospel of his son").

listes, didaskalos, prophetes, diakonos, presbuteros, episkopos—to mention only the most important words in the vocabulary. I need hardly add that they were not taken from the sacral world of Greece or Roman either. In fact, all the terms used in the apostolic writings for the "service" of the "gospel" and the *ekklesia* come directly from secular speech (which is not to say speech foreign to the "religious" world), though there may have been for a time a partial—and, in my opinion, completely accidental—analogy between the Christian *episkopos* and the *mebakker* of Qumran.

This is simply a fact, solid and evident too, as soon as one pauses to consider it. And this fact can have only one, equally all-embracing, significance: that those people who in early times served the "gospel" and the *ekklesia* did not think of themselves, nor were they thought of by the community, as a group who formed a "sacral caste," like the members of the Levitical priesthood. This is even more noteworthy when one considers that there was certainly no lack of models of this type, either in Judaism or in the Greco-Roman world. Quite the reverse: such models were obvious for all to see—all they had to do was to chose among them. As for the Levitical priesthood, in particular, any Jew who had become Christian must obviously have still had it under his skin, so to say. Nevertheless, the models were and remained unused, for some time at least, and that they were so can hardly have been just by chance; there was a reason, and one that it is still revelant to understand.

Though the "ministers of the word" (Lk 1 : 2) and of the community were not at first seen, either individually or collectively, as being endowed with any sacral quality thenceforth permanently attached to them as persons, it would be going too far to conclude from this simply that the first Christian communities dissociated themselves from everything connected with the world of the sacred, and felt alien to it. What seems to me truer to say, is that the first generations produced by the gospel were perfectly conscious of sacred rites and actions as a continuing part of their Christian life, but did not therefore extend that awareness to the point of bestowing a permanent and inalienable sacral character upon the actual persons who performed the gestures or presided over the rites.

The same attitude can also be observed in regard to the places and furniture used for worship. Thus the eucharist was first of all celebrated in houses which were simply the homes of those who welcomed the *ekklesia* into them: Prisca and Aquilas in Ephesus and Rome (1

Cor 19 : 19; Rom 16 : 5), Nymphas in Laodicea (Col 4 : 15), Philemon and Apphia in Colossae (Philemon 2). It was then found natural and fitting to celebrate the eucharist in a completely secular context, just as Jesus himself had eaten his last Passover meal in a private house in Jerusalem. It would be ridiculous, too, to suppose that the tables, cups, and other implements used in the celebration of the eucharist were from then on thought of as "altars" and "sacred vessels." On this point we must be careful not to be drawn along unthinkingly by the metaphors, comparisons, and analogies which we come upon here and there in the apostolic writings.[3]

The situation as a whole, both as regards the persons and as regards the things involved in worship, was one of tremendous simplification as compared with the sacral world of contemporary Judaism. That simplification was certainly also one of the chief factors that made it possible for the primitive church to break out of the limits of Judaism so as to become part of the vast world of the empire in the empire's own early and rapidly changing period. By lifting to some extent the burden of the sacred, the young church gained enormous flexibility for its structures as can at once be seen from the birth of absolutely new functions and services: apostles, evangelists, prophets, and prophetesses, presbyters, bishops, and deacons. Thereby the first Christian communities were also assured a very wide freedom of action, invention, and adaptation.

Paul felt most keenly that such flexibility of structures and such freedom of adaptation were necessary conditions for spreading the gospel beyond the original bounds of Judaism. But he cannot have been alone in thinking along these lines, although—as we know—there were reservations, hesitancies, objections, and even, with some, a straightforward harking back to the past. But the whole history of the time can only make sense if Paul's attitude on this point was, by and large, the attitude of the majority.[4]

---

[3] Especially, as regards the altar (1 Cor 9 : 13; 10 : 18; Heb 13 : 10). Again at the turn of the third century, Minutius Felix could list to his pagan interlocutors all the reasons why, he said, "we have neither temples nor altars" (*Octavius*, 23). In the same sense, Clement of Alexandria, *Stromata* VII, 6 (31, 8): "Our earthly altar is the assembly of those who give themselves to prayer, rooted so to say in a single voice and a single mind"; also Origen, *Contra Celsum* VIII, 17. However, at the same period we find in Tertullian (*De oratione* XIX, 3) the first appearance of the concrete sense of the word soon to become familiar to the whole church.

[4] Compare Jn 4 : 21–4: "Woman, believe me, the hour is coming when neither on this mountain nor in Jerusalem will you worship the Father . . ." We may

From our point of view, the Epistle to the Hebrews to some extent stands apart. It deals with a delicate question which must, in the first generation, have come to trouble many Christians of Jewish origin. The problem must particularly have disturbed those whose priestly background (Acts 6 : 7) turned their thoughts in the direction of the Temple and its liturgy of sacrifice. "It is evident," remarks the author, "that Our Lord was descended from Judah"; and it was equally evident to everyone that the law of Moses had given that tribe no part in serving "at the altar" (Heb 7 : 13-14). In these circumstances, what could have been, what could now be, the meaning of the Levitical priesthood when, in fact, the hope of "salvation" had arisen not from Levi but from Judah? These were roughly the terms in which the question presented itself.

The answer suggested by the author of the epistle puts forward several considerations, one of which is most directly of interest to us. The author's approach also strikingly recalls Paul's approach earlier to the more general problem of the relationship between the law and the freely-given justification which the "gospel of God" offers to all men without distinction through faith in the dead and risen Jesus, Christ and Lord. The law in there, it is true, explains Paul, but even before the law God had given us, in the person of Abraham, a model heralding another justice, better than the kind we obtain by fidelity to the law: a freely-given justice depending only on faith in Christ Jesus.

The author of Hebrews goes on to note that the sanctuary, the priesthood of Aaron, and the sacrifices are of course realities, but—he adds in substance—even before the priesthood of Aaron, God had given us, in the person of Malchizedek, a model heralding another higher and more perfect priesthood than that. And now, Jesus, Christ and Lord, has been given in his death and resurrection a better priesthood than that exercised of old in the Temple: "holy, blameless, unstained, separated from sinners," free of the necessity for daily repetition, since, in him, our sacrifice has been offered "once for all" and accepted by God (Heb 7 : 1-28). Jesus is "priest" (*hiereus*), he is our one "high priest" (*arkhiereus*) forever, "after the order of Melchizedek." If we add to this the tremendous idea that the whole church to which the gospel event gave birth formed a new "royal priesthood . . . [to] declare the wonderful deeds of him who called

---

also recall, in the same sense, the very important primitive idea of the "sacrifice of praise," the true center of Christian worship (Heb 13 : 15; *Didache* 14 : 3).

you" (1 Pet 2 : 9), then we possess all the essentials of our earliest heritage relating to the Christian "priesthood."

We can then gauge the distance between this new "priesthood," so simplified and "spiritualized," and the whole apparatus of the sacral with which the Aaronic priesthood was still surrounded. Basically, we may say that the simplicity of the new "priesthood" matched the simplicity of the new "sacrifice": naturally and of necessity, there was from the first a balance between the two. Thus it happened that though the church in its beginnings, had a multiplicity of "services," those services did not, properly speaking, constitute a "priestly hierarchy" comparable to the Levitical hierarchy, in which those responsible for the "services" became endowed with a permanent and inalienable sacred character. Furthermore, for several generations the church lived upon its original inheritance, without, it seems, any keen sense of needing to extend the area of the sacred in its pastoral structures. In its eucharist, it possessed a "sacrifice of praise" for the whole *ekklesia* (1 Pet 2 : 9, quoted above). Above all, it believed that in Jesus now present with the Father through his death and resurrection, it had a "high priest" with whose mediation no other had ever been, or could ever be, comparable.

Indeed it is not until the end of the second and beginning of the third centuries that we first glimpse any notable change in the church's life in this respect. The phenomenon is obviously extremely complex, and I certainly cannot analyze it adequately here; but it is still important to look at it briefly and see what its significance was.

The vocabulary of the time is our best indication of the profound changes then taking place in the mind of the church in regard to the pastoral "service." In fact, it was in the first half of the third century that the use of a "priestly" terminology began to spread alongside the older designations for the various "services" in the church. As far as we can judge, its use became widespread in an astonishingly short time, since we find it at about the same period simultaneously in Africa, Italy, Egypt, and Syria. Among the most important witnesses of the time we may mention here Tertullian, Cyprian, Origen, the *Traditio apostolica*, and the *Didascalia*. In them, the old "services," especially those of the *episkopos* and the *presbuteros*, have become— or become looked upon as—"priestly" services. *Episkopos, presbuteros, hiéreus, arkhiéreus*, and their Latin or Syriac equivalents, are freely interchanged, and it becomes evident, too, that the sense of the sacred which these titles suggested became extended, beyond the people themselves, to cover everything directly connected with their "service"—the places of assembly, the objects used in worship, and so on.

In the development then taking place, however, it seems to have been Cyprian of Carthage who took the lead, with the force, the richness, and the comparative novelty of his formulae. About a century and a half—scarcely five generations—had passed since the letter from Clement of Rome to the church in Corinth was written. Yet what a lot had changed! With Clement, the pastoral service, though often described as a *leitourgia*, was still defined first and foremost as a "service of Christ's flock"[5]—which had also been the most usual point of view in the previous generation: the *episkopos* had the "care" of "God's church" (1 Tim 3 : 5); his responsibility for it could be compared to that of the "shepherd" for his flock (Acts 20 : 28); the *presbuteros* is God's steward over the *ekklesia* (Tit 1 : 7).

Clearly, Cyprian was not rejecting any part of that inheritance of watchfulness and solicitude, either in theory or in his personal example. Yet there still remains the remarkable fact that Cyprian seems to have felt no hesitation in defining pastoral care, *first and foremost*, as a "service of the altar and sacrifices."[6] Such a view, still a novelty upon the third-century scene, undoubtedly marks a major change in the conception of the church's pastoral service. That service was, in effect, seen by Cyprian as a sacred function, a *ministerium sacrum*, whose obligations centered primarily on an "altar" where a "sacrifice" was offered. From that centre, the "altar of God,"[7] the sacred went out to communicate itself to the pastoral world as a whole,[8] and in

---

[5] I *Corinthians*, 44 : 3: *leitourgesantas amemptos toi poimnioi tou khristou*, in speaking of the bishops, or presbyters, whom the Corinthians had unjustly removed from their "service" (*leitourgia*). In the preceding sentence, Clement had used the same general term *leitourgia* to designate the apostolic "service" (44 : 2; compare Paul's phrase, quoted above: "minister [*leitourgon*] of Christ Jesus to the Gentiles [*eis ta ethne*]," Rom 15 : 16).

[6] *Letters* I, 1, 1. The letter condemns the action of Geminius Victor in making it a clause in his will that the priest Geminius Faustinus should be tutor to his children. Cyprian recalls, on the point, a well-established conciliar ruling that one must take neither a tutor nor a guardian from among "clerics and ministers of God," for those who have been "honoured by the divine priesthood" and established in the "ministry of the clergy" must take on no other "service than that of the altar and sacrifices" (*non nisi altari et sacrificiis deservire . . . debeant*), that they may keep themselves entirely for the prayer of the church. Similar formulae can be found elsewhere in the same letter: 1, 2; 2, 1; 2, 2; also XLIII, 5, 2; LIX, 18, 1; LXVII, 1, 2; LXXII, 2, 2.

[7] *Letters* I, 2, 1.

[8] *Letters* LXX, 1, 3; 2, 2.

doing so brought with it, as always, a certain characteristic development of sensitivity to the pure and impure.[9] Beyond the *ecclesia* there now extended the vast domain of the "profane," the "secular," of "perversion," of "uncleanness," of "sacrilege," where dwelt idolators, renegades, schismatics, and heretics, and where there could be no hope of salvation. Christian hope thus became wholly enclosed within the *ecclesia*, and the *ecclesia* in its turn was wholly impregnated with the purifying atmosphere engendered by the sacred.

It now becomes easy to see how the bishop, the *episcopus*, could so readily be described by Cyprian as a *sacerdos Dei*, and that those subordinate to him in the pastoral service should accordingly be designated as the *ministri Dei*. In each case the phrase expressed the perception of a certain sacral value corresponding to the fact that, in Cyprian's mind, the bishop and his assistants were first and foremost "at the service of the altar and of the sacrifices," and, seemingly, that it was by way of those sacrifices that the pastoral service was henceforth to identify its primary purpose within the *ecclesia*. In addition, the "clergy" were now, by the same token, subject to the distinctive demands generally imposed by proximity to the sacred—demands which were certainly unrecognized in that form, or to that extent, in the days when the pastoral service was primarily and immediately defined as a service of the *ekklesia*. Finally, as was hardly surprising in the circumstances, the distinctive requirements of the sacred came to be formulated in terms largely borrowed from the Old Testament. As Cyprian wrote:

Being all assembled after the council of the autumn of 254, we read, dearest brethren, the letter you sent us by our fellow bishops Felix and Sabinus, which bears witness to the integrity of your faith and the fear of God that is in you. In it you tell us that Basilides and Martialis, who have defiled themselves (*conmaculatos*) by issuing permits for idolatry, and who have abominable crimes on their conscience, must not exercise their episcopate nor fulfil the functions of the priesthood of God (*episcopatum gerere et sacerdotium Dei administrare non oportere*). You also express the wish to receive a reply on this matter, asking that our expressed opinion should bring you comfort or help in your just and necessary anxiety. But you already have the reply to your question, not so much in the results of our deliberations as in the commands of God. It has long been determined by heavenly statement and the law of God who they must be who take part in the service of the altar and

9 *Letters* LXV, 3, 3; LXVII, 1, 2; LXX, 2, 2; LXXII, 2, 2.

celebrate the divine sacrifices (*deservire altari et sacrificia divina celebrare*). In Exodus, indeed, God, speaking to Moses, warns him in these terms: That priests who draw near the Lord purify themselves (*sanctificentur*) lest the Lord reject them [19 : 22]. And again: When they draw near the altar of the Holy for their service, they must have no stain of sin upon them, lest they die [30 : 20, 21]. Similarly, in Leviticus, the Lord gives this command: The man who has a defilement and a sin upon him must not draw near to offer oblations to God [21 : 17].[10]

Spontaneously, there came a profound new awareness of the twofold value of the sacred and the pure to re-establish the continuity between the conditions for entering the pastoral service of the church, and some of the most characteristic rules which had in the past governed the exercising of the Levitical priesthood.

In this first half of the third century, then, the process of "sacralizing" the church's "services" got well under way. Obviously, however, it was as yet far from reaching every sector of that "service." Above all, it was still far from having produced all its consequences. Thus, for instance, the *Traditio apostolica* certainly speaks of the bishop's having a *primatus sacerdotii* (*arkhierateuein*), thus bringing together the two ideas of "leader" and "priest," but it does not yet say that after his "election" the bishop is "sacred," or "consecrated." It only speaks of him as "ordained" (which was, at first at least, a secular term). Nor did the ritual indicate any distinctive act of "consecration." All it in fact allowed for was a laying on of hands by all the bishops present, followed first by a silent prayer by the whole assem-

---

[10] *Letters* LXVII, 1. The same texts, quoted freely, are used elsewhere in reference to priests and deacons who have received a "profane ordination" (*profana ordinatione promoti*) outside the "Catholic church." "Priests and ministers engaged in the service of the altar and sacrifices," writes Cyprian, "must be without dishonour or stain (*integros atque inmaculatos*)." Then follow the three quotations we have seen (*Letters* LXXII, 2). It is important, in addition, to notice the close relationship between the text and two other Old Testament passages which Cyprian uses in order to promote the ideal of continence: "Similarly, in Exodus, God having commanded Moses to purify (*ut sanctificaret*) the people for three days, Moses purified them, adding: "Be ready by the third day; do not go near a woman" [19 : 15]. Similarly, in the First Book of Kings: And the priest answered David, "I have no common bread at hand, but there is holy bread (*sanctus panis*); if only the young men have kept themselves from women, [they can eat of it]" [1 Sam 21 : 5]. (*Testimonia* III, 32; Cyprian adds Rev 14 : 4.) From the fourth century on, these two examples were to assume the force of archetypes: and as such they were to contribute in great measure to the formulating of fresh requirements of conjugal continence first of all, and later of celibacy, for clergy engaged in the direct service of the altar and the *sacramenta*.

bly "for the descent of the Holy Spirit," and then by a prayer said aloud by one of the bishops present, who was once again to lay hands upon the "ordained" man. The spoken prayer naturally re-echoed the silent one: it asked primarily for all the gifts of the "Spirit" he would need to carry out his various functions. One need only read the text to see that there is absolutely no indication in it of any express intention to "consecrate." They were simply "ordaining," and at that time *ordination* had not yet come to signify *consecration* too.[11]

A century later, however, the idea of "consecration" seems to have advanced so far that it was taken for granted. Eusebius of Caesarea, for instance, writes:

> For those who have been consecrated (or, "made sacred": *hiero-menois*) and who have engaged themselves to serve God (*ten tou theou therapeian*), it is fitting to abstain afterwards from relations with their wives.[12]

In this last text, we should also note the idea of "consecration" being used as a reason for the "fittingness" of married abstinence. The higher services in the church constitute a *therapeia*, a "sacred service,"[13] Those who engage in the higher "services" are "consecrated" for that end: they are *hieromenoi* (or *hieratikoi*). And, adds Eusebius, it is "fitting" (*prosekei*) that those who accept "consecration" for such "service" should henceforth abstain from relations with their wives.

Eusebius was by no means the first in the church to propose this special form of continence. As we have already seen, the Council of Elvira, in about 300, actually made it a rule for bishops, priests, deacons, and generally for all clergy engaged in the "ministry" (canon 33). Such a rule was also to be proposed at the Council of Nicaea

---

[11] *Traditio apostolica*, II–III (ed. Dix, pp. 2–6). Dix speaks quite simply of "the sacred" and of "consecrating" the bishop, but he is making too big a jump. Things were far from being as clear-cut as that.

[12] Eusebius, *Demonstratio evangelica* I, 9. Similarly, canon 19 of the Council of Laodicea: "It is permitted only to consecrated ministers (*monois tois hieratikois*) to enter the sanctuary (*thusiasterion*) and receive communion there." We find the same absolute use of *hieratikos* in canon 24 to indicate clergy in major orders (down to and including the diaconate). As regards the encounter between the sense of the sacred and the world of sexuality, compare canon 44 already quoted): "Women must not enter the sanctuary (*thusiasterion*)." (Hefele-Leclerq 1, 2, 1010, 1012, and 1020.) We find the same terminology in Basil, *Letters* 104; and in Sozomen, *History of the Church* I, 23.

[13] More explicitly, further on in the text: *hierourgia*.

(325), but there, on the intervention of the bishop Paphnutius (of Thebais Prima, in Egypt), was rejected. However, what interests us here, far more than the question of chronological priority, is the reason put forward in the argument outlined by Eusebius. For this type of argument, which, though ostensibly depending on the perception of the "sacred," was in fact surreptitiously making use of the archaic distinction between "pure" and "impure," was to hold sway for a very long time. And in this instance the argument makes clear at least some of its sources—above all, it sought the explicit support of a comparison between the old "priesthood" and the new.

It was in this form that the argument was presented by Ambrose around the end of the fourth century (I give here the most important passage):

> You who have received the grace of the sacred ministry (*sacri minis-terii gratiam*), with an untouched body, an untainted modesty (*incorrupto pudore*), to whom also all conjugal relations are unknown, you know that you must be sure of an unhindered and spotless ministry (*inoffensum . . . et immaculatum*), which must not even be profaned by any conjugal relation (*nec ullo conjugali coitu violandum*). I have not wanted to pass over this matter in silence, for in many further-off places clerics have had children during the exercise of the ministry (*ministerium*), and even of the episcopate (*sacerdotium*). Furthermore, they defend their behaviour by citing the ancient custom, when the sacrifice was only offered at intervals. In truth, even the people purified themselves (*castificabatur*) for three or four days in order to come pure (*purus*) to the sacrifice, as we read in the Old Testament [Ex 19 : 10]. They also used to wash their clothes. But if their piety was so great in the time of prefiguring, what should not ours be in the time of the reality? Priest (*sacerdos*) and Levite, learn what it means to wash your clothes, in order to present a pure body to the sacraments you must celebrate (*ut mundum corpus celebrandis exhibeas sacramentis*). If the people [of Israel] were forbidden to take part in their offering without having washed their clothes, would you dare to offer for others with a defiled mind as well as a defiled body? Would you dare to act as their minister?[14]

It is obvious, first of all, that the terminology Ambrose uses here to speak of everything relating to pastoral "service" is not peculiar either to this passage, or to the writer of it. It is important to note here what

[14] Ambrose, *De officiis ministrorum* I, 50 (248).

is, from our point of view, its dominant characteristic: it is from beginning to end a sacral terminology. Its key pharses, with some others to be found elsewhere in the text, include: *minister Domini, ministerium, sacrum ministerium, ministrare, sacerdos, sacerdotium, levita* (=deacon), *officium levitarum.*

We see, further, what Ambrose's argument hinges on. It is the "ministry," precisely so far as it is seen to be "sacred," which requires a certain style, and even a certain state of life, in him who exercises it. Above all, the "ministry" excludes that "taint" upon the sacred which conjugal relations and the procreation of children must involve. This is followed by an example drawn from the Old Testament, and used earlier by Cyprian: in order to be "pure" when the time came to participate in the "sacrifice," the whole people observed continence, "purified themselves" for two or three days, and washed their clothes. But if there was such force of discipline and piety at the time of the figure, Ambrose concludes, what should it not be now that we have come to the reality?

It seems clear that Ambrose's ideas here are governed primarily by a certain perception of the sacred: in that perception it is as though the sacral character of the *sacramenta* spreads, through the "ministry" (*sacrum ministerium*), right to the actual person (*tu . . . mente pariter et corpore*) of him who has been "chosen" to celebrate them.[15]

Now we also know—because it is a common experience in the religious phenomenon as such—that such a perception of the sacred generally draws the "pure" into its obit as one of its conditions of existence and effectiveness. This certainly seems to be what has happened here: the awareness of being in the presence of the *sacramenta* of the church, exercising its drawing power on the "pure," forms for itself an ideal of "purity" of body and soul, which from then on seems to be its own normal condition of existence. In addition, and no less characteristically, since it is also not considered possible—given a basically ambivalent preconception of woman and of sexuality[16]— for that condition of "purity" to be fulfilled within marriage, only one

---

[15] You have therefore been chosen among the multitude of the children of Israel, you have appeared as the first born among the sacred fruits . . ."—and this is only the deacon! (*De officio ministrorum* 1, 50 (250).)

[16] Ambrose, *Exhortatio virginitatis* VI, 36: "Now indeed (that Adam has sinned, and Eve been stung by the serpent with the poison of lubricity), even though marriage is good, it nevertheless involves elements which make even the couple themselves blush together."

conclusion remains possible: the "sacred ministry" involves as a necessary consequence the rule of sexual abstinence, that is to say, of continence in all its forms, including—ultimately—celibacy. The circle is complete.

No one, I am sure, will believe that I am venturing upon this analysis for the malicious and imprudent pleasure of attacking the religious views of a great Christian and a great bishop. The importance of the issue at stake is too great for that. Moreover, Ambrose is here only one example cited from among many possible examples, whether from his own period or from the centuries that followed.[17]

---

[17] Among others, the important letter (decretal) from Siricius to Himerus of Tarragona (385): "Let us now come to the most sacred orders of clergy (*ad sacratissimos ordines clericorum*) . . . We have learnt that a great number of priests and deacons, long after their consecration (*post longa consecrationis suae tempora*), have begotten children, either by their own wives, or by some shameful union, and that they defend their crime by referring to that Old Testament text in which we read that priests and ministers were free to have children. Let him who has become a disciple of voluptuousness and master of vice tell me, then, if he considers that almost everywhere in the law of Moses the Lord gave free reign to lust for the sacred orders (*sacris ordinibus*), how it came about that this warning was given to those in charge of the holy of holies: You shall be holy, for I the Lord your God am holy (Lev 19 : 2). Let him further explain to me why it was enjoined upon priests to dwell in the Temple, away from their homes during the year of their service, if not for the reason that they should have no sexual relations (*carnale . . . commercium*) even with their wives. Thus they were able, in the glory of a clear conscience, to present to God an offering that was acceptable. Once the time of their service had expired, it was again permitted to them to use their wives, but only for the purpose of securing descendants, since the law declared that only the descendants of Levi should be admitted into the service of God. And the Lord Jesus also, when he enlightened us by his coming, declared in the gospel that he was not come to destroy the law, but to fulfill it. That is why he willed that the church, whose bridegroom he is, should shine with the splendour of chastity, that on the day of judgment, upon his return, he might find her without spot or wrinkle, are bound by the irrevocable law (*indissolubili lege*) of these provisions, in such a way that from the day of our ordination (*a die ordinationis*) we subject both our hearts and our bodies to sobriety and purity (*pudicitiae*), because we want to be totally pleasing to our God in those sacrifices we offer every day. But those who are in the flesh, says the Vessel of election, cannot please God. But you are no longer in the flesh but in the spirit, if the Spirit of God really dwells in you (Rom 8 : 9). And where can the Spirit of God dwell if not, as we read, in holy bodies?" (*PL* LVI, 558–9; partially in Denzinger-Schönmetzer 185.)

In the same sense, the letter (decretal) of Innocent I to Victricius of Rouen (404): "Whatever is worthy and conforms to modesty and chastity the church must absolutely preserve. Thus, let priests and deacons have no [sexual] relations with their wives, for they are engaged in the needs of a daily ministry. For it is written: You shall be holy, for I, the Lord your God am holy [Lev 19 : 2]." The letter then goes on to recall the example quoted above of the temporary continence imposed on the Levitical priesthood, and concludes: how much more then must

It has been necessary here to stress this one point which seems to have been generally overlooked in the history of the origins of ecclesiastical celibacy. But, though I have stressed it in this way, I do not by any means want to suggest that the progressive "sacralization" of the church's pastoral service from the end of the second century onwards, and the encounter between this general phenomenon of sacralization with the fundamental ambivalence of the sense that some "impurity" was almost inseparable from any manifestation of sexuality, constituted the sole reason for the establishment of ecclesiastical celibacy. What I do want to suggest is that they constitute a historical factor of the first importance. And it is evident, too, that this factor, though for most of the time buried in our collective unconscious, remains extremely active at the present time.

It does seem as if the powerful repulsion by the sacred of the impure seems to have played the decisive role here. That repulsion turned what had been at first conceived primarily merely as a particularly useful condition of liberty for the service of the word into a condition of "purity" felt to be, and later justified as being, necessary for the service of the altar and the *sacramenta*. The former was naturally expressed in the form of an invitation, and remained no more than a "suggestion" implicitly contained in concrete situations. But the latter, on the other hand, it would have been difficult not to turn into law. The former was flexible, easily allowing for varying ways of applying it, according as they might appear fruitful and fitting in relation to the service of the gospel. The latter made a once-for-all stand in favour of an invariable situation; it was rigid, and could not be otherwise, because it focused attention on the basic incompatibility between the impure and the sacred. As we have noted in passing, in this changeover, the rules of "purity" of the Levitical priesthood came in due course to provide a model which it seemed normal to follow,

---

the priests and deacons of the church preserve their purity from the day of their ordination, since for them there does not come a day when they have no longer to attend to the "divine sacrifices" and the ministry of baptism. If also Paul recommends (*praecipit*) laymen to abstain from their wives for a time in order to devote themselves to prayer, how much more should priests, whose permanent ministry is one of prayer and sacrifice, abstain at all times from such relations! "He who has been defiled (*contaminatus*) by sexual desire (*carnali concupiscentiae*), what shame shall be his when he turns to the sacrifice. By what power of inner persuasion, or by what merit can he believe his prayer heard?—for it is written: To the pure all things are pure, but to the corrupt and unbelieving nothing is pure [Tit 1 : 15]." (*PL* LVI, 523–4.)

though one which at the same time must be perfected. In this way the links with Judaism which, in the first generation of Christians, seemed to have been broken were in the end renewed, with grave ambivalences and by means of many and various equivocations.

It seems legitimate, however, to think that the present situation both in the church and in the world demands that we make a courageous and clear-sighted reappraisal of the whole matter.

We can begin by saying with complete assurance that the perception and religious evaluation of the "pure" and "impure," especially in the sphere of sexuality, are by no means specifically Christian. And it must be added, for the benefit of any who urge the example of the Levitical priesthood, that such a perception and evaluation are not in themselves peculiar to the Jewish tradition either. In fact, the perception of sexual "purity" and "impurity," as well as the very different evaluations placed upon it over the course of history, belong to the most archaic depths of human consciousness, where they are bound up with the most elementary structures of fear. The question is whether it is desirable for us to maintain those structures and cultivate that archaism indefinitely; whether the law of clerical celibacy, with all the very real it has produced, is to continue indirectly to stand surety for one of the most evidently regressive elements in our entire inheritance as human beings. Sexuality, whether of clergy or laity, will always be better served by justice, hope, and love than by all our obsessive concern with the "pure" and the "impure," which can ultimately only undermine its strength, its balance, and its beauty.

We can go on to say that, in our religious inheritance, not everything is on the same level, not everything is equally necessary or equally opportune. We must make a choice, or the course of history will inevitably make our choice for us. In the total view, what seems desirable is a lightening and a simplification—analogous, perhaps, to the stripping away by the first Christian generations of so much of the religious inheritence of Judaism in order to carry the gospel to the Greco-Roman world.

Much will depend, both in the choices the church can make and in the creations it can at the same time offer, on the judgement—whether expressed or only implicit—we have made on the religious situation of the world today. Can we be certain that our world is moving toward de-Christianization and irreligion? Myself, I often have a sense that it is moving in the first instance away rather from a multitude of religious forms left over from the past. But the sacred is not the divine. It is precisely when it seems to become identified with the divine that it degenerates, so that religion itself also degenerates and becomes simply magic. After all, Christianity recognizes but one mediator, and he is a person: Jesus, Christ and Lord, the Son of God.

Hence, it may be that what it remains for us to understand is that our Christianity cannot merely subsist but must in the future actually grow and develop, for the hope of mankind, in a world that sees itself as a purely profane one. Once we have understood that, then I think we shall also be able to understand that the pastoral service of the church has no absolute need for the apparatus of the sacred which early centuries have bequeathed to it. We shall be able also to understand that the consequences of that " sacralization" upon the style of life of the clergy are by no means necessary or unalterable, and that the whole of our hope for the future does not, after all, depend upon them.

6

Pastoral Service, Liturgical Assembly, and "Base Community"

Here we come to a network of extremely complex relationships. Perhaps we are not sufficiently aware of it, but in fact the actual existing structures of the relationship between "liturgical assembly" and "base community" are one of the defining and limiting factors on the situation of our "pastoral service" in the world as it is. And this limiting factor will be even tighter and stronger in the future if, as the demographers predict, the population of the world increases to between five and seven billion by the year 2000, and if—which is perhaps, from our present point of view, even more important—that world population is nine-tenths urban.

Even now, in towns, and even in many country districts—apart from such exceptions as mission areas and young churches—the "parish" has long ceased to coincide with the "liturgical assembly." Not merely do they not coincide now, but it is quite plainly impossible for them ever again to coincide in the future unless we resolve totally to remold the infrastructure of the church—in other words, of the "base community" in which the Christian life is normally born, developed, and worked out.

Here are some figures worth pondering on—they are in fact fairly well known to most of us. Countries where the average population in urban "parishes" does not exceed 5,000 are fortunate. This includes the East as well as the West. On the other hand, there are whole countries where that average rises to several tens of thousands. And it can only be by a habit born of centuries[1]—indeed, a habit firmly based on the established order of things—that we have come to judge this situation as the "natural and normal" one. I would, on the contrary, make bold to say that it is a situation that is against nature and wholly abnormal for Christians. And I would go on to add that if there is a crisis in the pastoral service of our day—a crisis of recruitment, a crisis of effectiveness in preaching, even a crisis of perseverance for those engaged in the service—that crisis is largely, though not of course wholly, due to this very situation, a situation which, I must repeat, concerns the actual existing structure of the "base community."

I am not forgetting that, in some countries at least, in the past few decades there has been a "direct action on the milieu" which has come to the aid of the "parish." That action has to some extent succeeded, and in doing so, has produced some admirable Christians, by means of whom the gospel witness has been carried to places where the pastoral service of the "parish" could no longer penetrate. It has also brought notable support to the present renewal of the pastoral theology of the parish and of the liturgy. I am far from wishing to minimize the contribution made by this "direct action on the milieu," still less to propose any reduction of it. But if one asks whether our experience to date gives us any reasonable hope that "direct action on the milieu" will eventually succeed in remedying all the cumbersomeness and ineffectiveness of the parish institution, then one must surely say: No—even supposing that it could be better coordinated in the near future with a pastoral renewal in the parishes.

First of all, "direct action on the milieu," conceived and carried out by lay people, leaves virtually untouched the central problem of the place and function of the priest in the parish institution, which is a problem of a quite different nature. And, secondly, it is by no means certain that what may be won, from the Christian point of view, by "direct action on the milieu" will also, and automatically, be won for the "parish" as such. There is a distance between the milieu and the parish which, in the present state of things, can hardly be called easy to bridge. Far from it. One cannot therefore help fearing that ultimately we shall be faced with a "direct action on the milieu" whose final effectiveness will be constantly compromised by a parish institution which has already been rejected as unfitting and ineffective as

[1] Since the fourth century, in fact, if we take a total view of both East and West.

regards that milieu. Shall we in fact always have to turn back at this point? Must it remain a dead end?

In the immediate postwar years the experiment of the priest-worker movement represented a further attempt to break out of the limitations of the parish institution, and find a new way round to reach certain specific milieux. I should be sorry indeed if I seem to make a summary judgement here upon an enterprise which was admirable in so many ways. But I must be brief, while having also to say honestly what I think. In spite of a profound sympathy for the movement, I personally always considered that it by-passed the real problem—or, rather, perhaps that the priest-workers took with them into the working-class world the still unresolved problem of the parish institution which they were leaving. It was certainly not part of their brief to deal with such a problem, nor had they the total vision, or the historical knowledge to do so. But their failure, understandable though it was, did nothing to change fundamentals. Thus the difficulties the movement was faced with increased, both from within and from without, and so, in the end, the cessation of the movement can be said to have marked a return to the more generally accepted ideas which still sustain the institution of the parish.

Perhaps I may, once again, stand back a little in order to try and evaluate the present situation more accurately. In the first place, what I should want to say from this slightly distanced vantage point is that, at the beginning, and indeed for some centuries,[2] there was always and for all practical purposes an identity between the litgurical assembly on the one hand and the base community—in other words, the local "church"—on the other. In apostolic times, indeed, this is clear from the fact that, at least in Greek-speaking places, the same word *ekklesia* was used for both the liturgical assembly and the local church. In my opinion there are also good reasons for thinking that the local church was called *ekklesia* for the very reason that it found its first and most natural expression in a "liturgical assembly" which was what the *ekklesia*, strictly speaking, meant. Leaving aside for the moment the other possible meanings superimposed on this one, that *ekklesia* which constituted the liturgical assembly was in fact not just "convoked" or "summoned," but literally "invited" and "welcomed" within the general framework of the customs and ceremonies of the

---

[2] The change began—but it was only a beginning—during the fourth century, with the building of the great city churches, of which the basilicas of the age of Constantine are the prime example.

domestic hospitality of the time. Thus, not merely was there virtually an identity between the "church" and the liturgical assembly, but also—which is no less important from both the sociological and the pastoral point of view—that identity existed in the context of home and family, with the customs and ceremonies of hospitality already established there.

That, then, was where our "church" was born; there also, for a long time, it lived and developed. The names of a few of those who "welcomed" the "church" in this way into their homes at the beginning are known to us from Paul's epistles: in Rome, Prisca and Aquila (Rom 16 : 3); the same couple in Ephesus (1 Cor 16 : 19); in Laodicea, Nymphas (Col 4 : 15); Philemon and Apphia in Colossae (Philemon 2). With these facts of history we are all fairly familiar, even if we are not too clear about the details and implications. What chiefly strikes me, however, is that we have not in general given enough thought to their bearing on pastoral theology, or to what they might have to tell us in regard to our own present situation. Therefore the comments that follow are in the nature of a short examination of these two points.

First of all we must say something on the question of numbers—crucial today, and probably even more so in the near future. Many people, I believe, imagine that the "churches" of the apostolic era were fairly large in number, though there are many who are content to leave the matter open. But it is worth at least trying to get some clear idea.

We do not, of course know, nor will we ever know, the number of Christians, say at about the year 60, in the town of Ephesus. Nor is it important that we should. On the other hand, we do know something of the size and shape of the average house of the time in the Greco-Roman world. We can thus obliquely arrive at some idea—approximate of course, but not wholly inaccurate—of the *ekklesia* which met together for the "word" and the "eucharist" in the home of Prisca and Aquila (1 Cor 16 : 19). They were people of the artisan class, and certainly did not have a nobleman's villa. We will not, I think, be far from the truth in putting the number of the church there at fifty.[3]

We find this figure indirectly confirmed from another direction.

---

[3] Compare Acts 20 : 7–8: the "upper chamber" in Troas, where Paul, passing through, presided over an assembly "on the first day of the week," that is, on Sunday.

There were religious associations in the pagan world of the time which were, so to speak, sociological analogues of the Christian *ekklesia*. These "fraternities"—*thiasoi, eranoi*, etc.—were never very large: some *thiasoi* had no more than ten or fifteen members, while others might number thirty, forty, fifty, or sixty in membership. The highest figure known to us is that of a *thiasos* in Attica, which had a membership of ninety-three (fifty-nine men and thirty-four women; in the second century BC). In Paul's day, in the towns of the Mediterranean basin, there was thus a long tradition of this sociological type of "assembly." In fact, taken together, the indications we can muster from the writing of the apostolic era suggest very definitely that the first Christian liturgical assemblies (*ekklesiai*) did not generally exceed the modest proportions dictated, not only by their domestic context, but also, it is important to remember, by the chief forms of the "word" ("message" and "instruction," *kerugma* and *didakhe*) on the one hand, and by the very symbolism of the "Lord's supper" on the other—not to mention the "breaking of bread" where that was the practice (probably in Palestine and Syria).

Moreover, it must not be thought that this situation altered very rapidly, at the end of the apostolic era, as the gospel impinged on ever larger sections of the Greco-Roman world. Quite the reverse: the evolution was a relatively slow one, a fact significant in itself. We may look briefly here at just a few pieces of evidence: the house-church (*domus ecclesiae*) of Doura-Europos[4] was no more than a house like any other, made over to the local church, and gradually arranged to suit the needs of the Christian community (first half of the third century). Its largest room, formed by knocking down an interior wall (about 232 AD) measured about 40 ft. by 16 ft., and could hold little more than sixty people; thus the situation was much the same as in the early days—apart, that is, from the alterations, and the consequent fixing of one regular meeting place for the "assembly."

Dura was not, of course, a very large town, and it would be unwise to set too much significance upon its *domus ecclesiae* from this particular point of view. But, at about the same time, the Syrian author of the *Didascalia* seems to have known only bishops who could, and for the most part did, still reserve to themselves personally the direct responsibility for distributing help to the needy members of their churches. He tells us what the reason was for this custom, and it is that reason which is most illuminating from our point of view: it was

---

[4] At the eastern frontier of the Empire, on the Euphrates.

because "the bishop indeed knows well those who are in difficulties."[5] This makes it abundantly clear that the Syrian bishops in the third century still generally presided over the lives of small "churches"—so small, indeed, that they normally knew each member by name.

As we noted in passing, even the fourth century did not bring such radical or such universal changes as the conventional picture we generally have of it might suggest. The most significant feature of the changes, from our point of view, is of course the more and more frequent use of the basilical plan in the building of new churches, and especially of city churches, in the first quarter of the fourth century. It was a plan with a long history in civil architecture, and a name suggestive of majesty: it was "kingly," "regal," with all the connected ideas of triumph and grandeur. There can be no doubt that the Basilica of the Holy Sepulcher in Jerusalem, to take one example, was an attempt to express just such ideas in stone.[6]

But a basilica commemorating the death and resurrection of Jesus in the very place where the things happened was of course *sui generis*. It must not be thought that all the basilicas that arose all over the empire in the fourth and fifth centuries were attempting to imitate or compare with that. Nonetheless, the basilical plan—whose prototype was taken from civil architecture, though there were some private "basilicas"—of itself introduced into the "base community" (the "diocese," and later the "parish") a seed which was to grow imperceptibly into what we now have today: the great church, not just a meeting place, but also a sign and symbol of the great assembly.

The essence of the phenomenon was that a move was already being made, and was to be made more and more commonly, away from the primitive prototype of the meeting place for the *ekklesia*, the ordinary home. Simultaneously, the base community was in future to carry within itself the seed of many various and profound changes which were, in time, to affect the faithful as well as the pastoral service itself. For the increase that took place in dimensions and numbers led to such a total change as to alter the character of the relationships of the base community, both within itself and with the world outside it. It was a movement from one sociological prototype to another: from a

---

[5] *Didascalia apostolorum* IX (25).

[6] Letter from Constantine to Macarius, Bishop of Jerusalem, in Eusebius, *Vita Constantini* III, 30–31. Despite all the bombast, it is interesting too to read the panegyric pronounced by that same Eusebius, Bishop of Caesarea, on the occasion of the opening of the new church of Tyre in about 317 (*History of the church* X, 4).

"fraternal" prototype, for which the home—and later the *domus ec-clesiae*—was at once the natural context and the true symbol, to a "crowd" prototype, for which the basilica rapidly, and almost throughout the empire, became the new context and symbol. The consequences of this movement were to be incalculable, as regards both the internal structure of the liturgical assembly and the various pastoral functions. A new style of ecclesial life was to make its appearance, and to that extent an equally new style of Christian life.

It goes without saying, of course, that those consequences were not at first obvious, still less were they at first recognized by those concerned. Furthermore, throughout the fourth and fifth centuries, a great part of the old order of things remained as it was, thus masking the changes. The continuance of habits, customs, and rules softened the transition, while making it possible to believe that everything was going on as before. Here it is also significant that even the "churches" which provided themselves with a basilica in the fourth century often placed the new assembly room among the complex of "houses" which were previously the vital center of the *domus ecclesiae*. There too, then, the transition could come about without anyone's at first realizing what its consequences would be.

The vocabulary used is a good witness here. In the fourth and fifth centuries, the "church" was not just the large building which was the special place of "assembly" (eventually the "basilica"), but also all the houses directly connected with it: the bishop's house (Augustine), the houses of the priests and other clergy—the deacons and sub-deacons engaged in the service of the "church"—the *secretarium*, and so on. Often enough, if not as a general rule, the new basilica came simply as part of the existing *domus ecclesiae*, which was, in any case, already to some extent especially arranged for its functions (in some places more than in others).

Here again, the figures are instructive from our point of view. The basilica of Hippo, recently brought to light by excavation,[7] may be considered a good example of the large urban churches of fourth- and fifth-century Africa. It was a building 66 ft. wide by 138 ft. long (161 ft. including the apse). On great occasions, the basilica might perhaps have held 2,000 people.[8] There would have been more than one celebration there, however; on ordinary days, even Sundays, it is quite certain that the "assemblies" must have been very much smaller. As

---

[7] Probably the actual basilica of Augustine.
[8] The population of the town was somewhere between 30,000 and 40,000.

for the churches in the surrounding countryside (in small towns, villages, or simply estates), they must have been nothing but "ecclesiolae" compared with the basilica of the episcopal city. Augustine always had plenty of clergy of all orders to serve his church—in 424, for instance, three priests, five or six deacons, and several subdeacons, not to mention lectors and other minor clerics for whom we have no precise figures. Three years later, the church of Hippo had no less than seven priests to serve it, who had been trained over the years in the bishop's own "house."

This brief glance is enough to indicate the distance that still lay, at the beginning of the fifth century, between a church like that of Hippo, and our own city "parish." Yet the church of Augustine was not in this respect out of the ordinary, and a similar situation prevailed in both the East and the West. What must in fact be said is that the modern parish—and particularly the large city parish, which displays sometimes almost to the point of a dismal caricature the features common to this sort of "base community"—is a relatively recent phenomenon in the church. It is therefore pointless, anachronistic, and—in my opinion—absolutely misleading for us nowadays to talk and think of the parish as though that institution starts with the advantage of having the whole of the church's pastoral tradition behind it—as if, therefore, it, and it alone, has a position of such privilege that it can never be touched or altered.

On the contrary, historical truth obliges us to say that it has nothing of the kind. I am convinced that our pastoral tradition—if we look at the breaks in it as well as the authentic continuity—does make it possible for us today to look at the present situation with the objectivity needed for a true view, rather than simply to be slaves of our own time. A living tradition must always be free to go on creating afresh in the future. Otherwise, under the appearances of continuity and fidelity, there only exists at best an honorable sclerosis, and ultimately perhaps a respectable death.

This being said, if one must give a brief characterization of the two great periods of our pastoral tradition as regards the fundamental conception of the "base community," I think one might put forward the following observations.

It would appear that, from the fourth and fifth centuries onwards, the base community of ecclesial life gradually gave up being modelled on the social prototype of the home and at the same time adopted a different model, that of the crowd. The most telling historical symbol of that change from one sociological prototype to another is to be found in the architecture: it was the slow, and almost universal, triumph of the basilical plan (and all its minor derivatives) over the old *domus ecclesiae*. It is thus most significant that our present-day churches are, for all practical purposes, "public buildings"; for it was this that their architecture was designed to make them become.

It would further appear that, in proportion as a new sociological prototype was adopted, from the fourth and fifth centuries onwards, the pastoral service itself turned from a system in which the (virtual) identity of the "liturgical assembly" and the "base community" was seen as natural and normal, to one in which that identity became, by force of circumstance and the fact of large numbers, harder and harder to achieve, difficult to maintain, and in the end altogether impossible. The primarily territorial nature of our parishes, and the enforced multiplication of the same services in the same churches on the same days, can be seen in this context as so many extremely illuminating symbols of the ground that has been covered, and the direction in which it has been covered, since the turn of the fourth century.

It would, finally, appear that the primitive pastoral system which chose spontaneously to adapt the dimensions and structures of the "base community" to the intrinsic possibilities of the forms of the word and of worship, was succeeded, from that same period, by a pastoral system which sought, ever more ineffectively, ever more hopelessly, to do the opposite—to adapt the forms of the word and of worship to the ever increasing dimensions, and the more and more complex and vague structures, of the "base community." For historical signs we have, for the "word," the development of "sacred eloquence" in place of the original "message" and "instruction," and, for "worship" properly so-called, the progressive reduction of the sacramental signs, especially those of the eucharist, which was once the true center of both pastoral service and Christian liturgy.

The "message" and "instruction" of the apostles were, in effect, intended to meet the individual as such within the framework of a "base community" similar in size to the family structure of the time. In particular, the sociological prototype for the "instruction" was drawn from the old family custom whereby the father would transmit "instruction" to his children when they reached the age of the "knowledge of good and evil" (adolescence). With an express reference to this custom of education in the home, Paul wrote of his own "instruction":

> You know how, like a father with his children, we exhorted each one of you (*hena hekaston humon*), and encouraged you and charged you to lead a life worthy of God, who calls you into his own kingdom and glory. [1 Thess 2 : 11–12; compare Acts 20 : 20–21.]

How often, in our sermons, we recall the Lord's table and the Last Supper (1 Cor 10 : 4; 11 : 20). Yet every priest and every layman knows that this is a far cry from actually feeling that one is at that "table," eating that "supper" in hope and faith and brotherly love. Many different factors, especially the size and structure of our base community, have gradually led us, or forced us, to minimize our eucharistic signs. There is a comparison I have often used in speaking of this. If you entertain a small number of relations or friends, you seat them at your table and serve them yourself with the best food you can provide; if you entertain twenty-five people, with whom you are connected in various ways, you would probably provide a cold buffet; if you entertain fifty people, even more variously connected, you would probably arrange a different time, and serve only "refreshments"; if you entertain two hundred people, you might possibly provide a meal, but if so, you would employ a professional caterer, and you yourself would manage to greet only a few of your guests individually, perhaps making a little speech of greeting to the assembled company. And so on—this comparison certainly makes my point clear, and perhaps I should apologize for making it quite so brutally clear. But what I want to stress is the fact that numbers are bound to dictate the form and content of human relationships. That is a law from which there is no escaping, especially perhaps in that most delicate pastoral area of the "word" and "sacraments."

If these observations are substantially correct, we come to the real problem that faces us; it is not primarily one of ultimately revising the methods of training and teaching now in force in our seminaries, though such a revision may well be desirable in itself. Nor is it primarily one of a better adaptation of the methods current in the parochial ministry, though that may be all that we can do for the moment. Nor is it primarily one of intensifying our "direct action on the milieu" in order to make up for inadequacy of the parish institution, though such an intensification would undoubtedly contribute enormously to the groundwork for the ecclesial forms of the future.

No, the real problem we are faced with relates to the dimensions and structures of the "base community." For without a thriving root, nothing can live. The form and content of our pastoral relationships will always very largely depend on what that "base community" is like. And one thing seems quite certain: the anonymity, the indifference, the dissatisfaction and sometimes even despair, which bedevil so much of our pastoral relationships today, both from the lay side and the clerical, will not disappear miraculously tomorrow because of our exhortations to fervor, to fidelity, to virtue, or to unselfishness. Something much more daring and much more creative is needed: God grant that we may be prepared to let it happen.

All I can do here is to make suggestions—nor have I ever sought to do more. However, within that restricted purpose, I trust that I may be permitted to speak in all honesty.

In the first place, as we have said so often, what seems needed is a clear-sighted and courageous reconsideration of the dimensions and structures of our base community. There were several centuries when things were different from what they are now. And it would seem especially desirable in this respect for us to take inspiration from the old *domus ecclesiae*, in order to set us free, if need be, from the slaveries and burdens of history. Nor is it a question of trying to put the clock back, but rather of seeking to rediscover our own tradition in greater fullness, and gain from it liberating hints and indications for the future.

By making the *domus ecclesiae* a model once more, I am not of course suggesting that we close our great churches, with all their long inheritance as the descendants of the fourth- and fifth-century creations. What I would like to see is the creation of an "assembly" (*ekklesia*) midway between the family and the kind of large "congregation" we know today. The principle upon which that *ekklesia* would be formed would be the old custom whereby the "liturgical assembly" and the "base community" virtually coincided.

Such an intermediate "assembly" could then be considered as our true "base community"—flexible, mobile, diversified, and at grips with the realities of human life. Its sociological basis would be the natural groups that grow up round a family—its close relations, neighbours, friends, those it helps and is helped by, its companions in work and leisure. As for the ideal number, such an "assembly" should be of a suitable size to meet in an ordinary home, whose dimensions would vary from place to place.

In this way we could get back to the ancient custom of adapting the "assembly" to the inherent possibilities of our forms of worship, rather than trying to adapt the forms of worship to the "assembly." Long-established custom, enshrined in our rubrics and in our buildings, has made us forget too readily that our forms of worship—especially those which constitute our eucharist and all that goes with it—came into existence for the most part within the restricted framework of home and family. Jesus celebrated his last Passover in an "upper room," where he followed all the customs of ordinary "hospitality."[9] We forget, too, that our chief forms of worship, by reason of their origins and their very nature, are not susceptible of being indefinitely extended, nor, therefore, of being indiscriminately adapted to any size or structure of gathering.

This would also mean providing the new base community with its own liturgy. It would be totally inadequate here to think of simply scaling down the liturgy in use for "big congregations." Our pastoral tradition, once we understood it better, would make it possible for us to create liturgical forms suited to the worshiping group we want. In that liturgy, the pastoral "welcome," so important both in expressing brotherly love and in actually forming the "assembly," would once again be given full scope. We know only too well how difficult that kind of "welcome" has become in our huge churches; indeed, that difficulty may be the first factor in producing a sense of isolation around the priest, so that a gulf is created between him and those for whom he is responsible as pastor. We must have the courage to recognize the fact that, though unwittingly and unintentionally, it is actually the forms of our liturgy that do most to make and maintain that separation between us.

Along with its own liturgy, this "base community" would also naturally need its own form of pastoral service—a service which would obviously be of a very extensive kind. Now it is precisely here that I think the present problem of celibacy in the church's pastoral service appears as most genuinely and urgently a problem. I can see no solution to it other than a straightforward and universal return to the freedom of primitive times. We are in no position to theorize

9 Compare 1 Tim 3 : 2, and Tit 1 : 8, on the need for the *episkopos* to be hospitable.

about what would be best in itself: the issue is whether we are in any position even to respond to the present needs of the church. Despite splendid and still immense reserves of inventiveness and generosity, we have to recognize that we are being overwhelmed on all sides. And, as far as we can foresee, our pastoral needs will be even greater in the future: they must take priority over everything else, and our choices, and decisions must be governed by them. After all, that seems to have been how Jesus himself judged the matter when calling his diciples and choosing the Twelve.

Finally, we could work out various ways of coordinating the functions of the new base community with the "large congregation," in relation both to liturgy and to the division of pastoral responsibilities. Such a redesigning of the ecclesial infrastructure would surely be feasible without any very great upheavals—in particular, without destroying the genuine values proper to the large congregation. We do, after all, have very good historical warrant for doing this in pastoral tradition itself: the parish as we know it is the result of a gradual transfer of responsibilities away from the bishop's cathedral church, under just the same kind of pressure of new needs. What I am here suggesting is a transfer of pastoral responsibilities, similar to what has already happened in the past, to the new "base community." With this difference, however, that we must not let the change take a thousand years to accomplish. Indeed, there are innumerable men and women, to all of whom God offers the good news of hope for life, for whom it may already be too late. Time presses. Should not our love for our brothers press us too, and in the same direction?

Conclusion

The awareness of how much is still to be said makes me somewhat reluctant to conclude. But we have all the same arrived at a few useful assurances. By and large, the results of our analyses would seem to banish once and for all the facile notion, expressed by some, but certainly assumed by a good many more, that the reasons which led the Latin church in the past to introduce the law of celibacy for the clergy, are adequate today to justify and perpetuate it.

Such a rose-colored view seems to me to be supported neither by the facts of history, nor by present circumstances. Nor could it be held for long by any save those who are convinced, without actually examining it, that they have an innate knowledge of the church's pastoral tradition, and that from this vantage point they can look down from above upon the march of history. Their hearts may be in the right places, but uncritical goodwill is not always enough. Honesty and modesty serve us better here, I think; and they would lead us to be prudent enough to investigate any question before pronouncing upon it, and then to recognize, if need be, whatever changes of perspective may result from changes of circumstance.

In fact, there are many of us, both clergy and laity, whose outlook on life is no longer such that we perceive any inherent "impurity" in the expression of sexuality. And for the future, one needs no especial prophetic insight to foresee that mankind as a whole is gradually moving, slowly but inevitably, towards a complete elimination of this spiritual archaism.

If my interpretation of the facts is substantially correct, there can be no doubt that it was something more than just "reasons" that led in the past to the establishment of celibacy as obligatory in the higher echelons of the church's pastoral service. There have been many more obscure energies at work as well. It may even be thought, without doing injustice to the conscience of Christian antiquity, that those energies were in this case the primary and determining factor, and that the "reasons" put forward in support of the law of ecclesiastical celibacy were useful chiefly in masking an area of consciousness moved by forces of a very different kind, arising directly out of the old sense of sexual "impurity."

It is thus primarily the fact of this particular conjuction of energies and "reasons" which poses the real problem regarding the deeper motives which underlie the enforcement of clerical celibacy in the present-day mind. This very ambiguous conjunction involves a number of unfortunate elements, some at least of which seem at the moment quite irremovable—particularly certain misinterpretations of the Bible, and the religious significance given to the sense of what is "pure" and "impure" in the sexual sphere. Nor does the fact that this conjunction has become to a greater or lesser degree masked by rational motives superimposed upon it over the course of time mean that it no longer exists, or that it has lapsed into a reassuring state of inactivity and become overgrown by the institution. It still exists and is still active, though it is true that its activity varies in degree from one individual and one group to another.

More precisely, it was the encounter between two perceptions— that of the sacred on one hand, and that of the "pure" and "impure" on the other—that was the most active and telling factor in the development which ended by producing the law of ecclesiastical celibacy. All the other factors—the regulations of the old Jewish priesthood, the witnesses and examples from early Christian tradition, the influence of the newer monasticism, the aspirations of the clergy themselves towards an ideal of "the common life"—seem by and large to have played only a supporting role. Certainly, unless we try to reconstruct history rather differently from what it really was, it is very unlikely that of themselves they would have led to any thing more than the optional regime which in fact is what existed in the church during its first three centuries.

Yet a law did come into being. And, from this viewpoint, it is once again the profound underlying dynamic of that law which poses the problem today—a problem primarily pastoral in character. For we must recognize that, by letting the pastoral service become totally sacralized, we have, by the same token, cut from under us most of the ordinary possibilities of adapting it to the changing circumstances of time, place, individuals and societies, cultures and civilizations. You cannot accept an out-and-out sacralization and at the same time hope to preserve all your likely chances of being part of the living moment of history. The reason for this is clear: the "sacred" will always try to assume the greatest possible immutability in order to safeguard its own special function.

Once again the facts force us to make a choice. All our experience of history shows that it would be utterly paradoxical to try to preserve unchanged a totally "sacralized" pastoral service while hoping at the same time to see the gospel go forward in step with the general movement of history. As we have cause to know, if the "sacred" remains too heavy a burden, it will slow us down all the time. However hard we may try, we cannot help missing every turning. And, in the last analysis, this is therefore the main context in which we must see the problem of the motives for clerical celibacy. For it is a law that harmonizes extremely well with a wholly sacralized pastoral service; yet it is by no means certain that such a service is in the best interests of the hope of the gospel.

Nor must we forget that the law of celibacy can quote very different reasons for its existence now from those which presided over its birth. Some people, aware perhaps of some of the difficulties we have been considering here, have set out to find one "absolute" motive which would allow of no hesitation. Above all, they have argued from the example of Jesus himself. This is, of course, something of supreme and enduring importance which transcends all the vicissitudes of time and change. Yet we can hardly fail to observe, as regards the question we are dealing with here, that the loftier the motive becomes, the harder it is to see it as the basis for a law. And in fact Jesus himself did no more than offer a choice: he suggested, he invited, but he did not oblige. You cannot make an absolute law for life. We solve one difficulty only by falling into another.

Is there a possibility that we shall honestly reconsider our law of clerical celibacy in the near future? It seems to me that we can only hope so. If we do, then the extraordinarily fruitful example of the pastoral service of the early church, with its integration of marriage into the whole family framework of the *ekklesia*, will at once become of enormous creative value in showing a way forward for the world of the future. We should see a pastoral service come into being whose first purpose would not be to adapt itself to some once-for-all, unchanging ideal of the "sacred," but to supply the needs of the gospel as they arise, in a wise and watchful liberty. We should see the leaven able once more to lighten every part of the lump.

Index of Sources and References